ALL ACCESS

A 365 Day backstage pass to the Kingdom

Written by Erika Collins

One year bible reading plan used with permission by
http://www.oneyearbibleonline.com/readingplan/oneyearbiblereadingplan.pdf

All Access Pass

Today's passages:

Genesis 1:1-2:25

Matthew 1:1-2:12

Psalms 1:1-6

Proverbs 1:1-6

What verse spoke to you in this reading?

Do the New Testament and Old Testament passages have any similarities?

What other verses come to mind as you read these passages?

What questions do you still have? What do you want to know more about? What lesson or theme are you picking up on?

How can you apply these scriptures to your life? -

Today's prayers:

All Access Pass — Day 2

What verse spoke to you in this reading?

Do the New Testament and Old Testament passages have any similarities?

What other verses come to mind as you read these passages?

What questions do you still have? What do you want to know more about? What lesson or theme are you picking up on?

How can you apply these scriptures to your life? -

Today's prayers:

Today's passages:

Genesis 3:1-4:26

Matthew 2:13-3:6

Psalms 2:1-12

Proverbs 1:7-9

Notes

All Access Pass — Day 3

Today's passages:

Genesis 5:1-7:24

Matthew 3:7-4:11

Psalms 3:1-8

Proverbs 1:10-19

What verse spoke to you in this reading?

Do the New Testament and Old Testament passages have any similarities?

What other verses come to mind as you read these passages?

What questions do you still have? What do you want to know more about? What lesson or theme are you picking up on?

How can you apply these scriptures to your life? -

Today's prayers:

All Access Pass — Day 4

Today's passages:

Genesis 8:1-10:32

Matthew 4:12-25

Psalms 4:1-8

Proverbs 1:20-23

Notes

What verse spoke to you in this reading?

Do the New Testament and Old Testament passages have any similarities?

What other verses come to mind as you read these passages?

What questions do you still have? What do you want to know more about? What lesson or theme are you picking up on?

How can you apply these scriptures to your life? -

Today's prayers:

All Access Pass — Day 5

Today's passages:

Genesis 11:1-13:4

Matthew 5:1-26

Psalms 5:1-12

Proverbs 1:24-28

Notes

What verse spoke to you in this reading?

Do the New Testament and Old Testament passages have any similarities?

What other verses come to mind as you read these passages?

What questions do you still have? What do you want to know more about? What lesson or theme are you picking up on?

How can you apply these scriptures to your life? -

Today's prayers:

All Access Pass — Day 6

Today's passages:

Genesis 13:5-15:21

Matthew 5:27-48

Psalms 6:1-10

Proverbs 1:29-33

What verse spoke to you in this reading?

Do the New Testament and Old Testament passages have any similarities?

What other verses come to mind as you read these passages?

What questions do you still have? What do you want to know more about? What lesson or theme are you picking up on?

How can you apply these scriptures to your life? -

Today's prayers:

All Access Pass — Day 1

Today's passages:

Genesis 16:1-18:15

Matthew 6:1-24

Psalms 7:1-17

Proverbs 2:1-5

What verse spoke to you in this reading?

Do the New Testament and Old Testament passages have any similarities?

What other verses come to mind as you read these passages?

What questions do you still have? What do you want to know more about? What lesson or theme are you picking up on?

How can you apply these scriptures to your life? -

Today's prayers:

All Access Pass — Day 8

What verse spoke to you in this reading?

Do the New Testament and Old Testament passages have any similarities?

What other verses come to mind as you read these passages?

What questions do you still have? What do you want to know more about? What lesson or theme are you picking up on?

How can you apply these scriptures to your life? -

Today's prayers:

Today's passages:

Genesis 18:16-19:38

Matthew 6:25-7:14

Psalms 8:1-9

Proverbs 2:6-15

Notes

All Access Pass — Day 9

Today's passages:

Genesis 20:1-22:24

Matthew 7:15-29

Psalms 9:1-12

Proverbs 2:16-22

Notes

What verse spoke to you in this reading?

Do the New Testament and Old Testament passages have any similarities?

What other verses come to mind as you read these passages?

What questions do you still have? What do you want to know more about? What lesson or theme are you picking up on?

How can you apply these scriptures to your life? -

Today's prayers:

All Access Pass — Day 10

What verse spoke to you in this reading?

Do the New Testament and Old Testament passages have any similarities?

What other verses come to mind as you read these passages?

What questions do you still have? What do you want to know more about? What lesson or theme are you picking up on?

How can you apply these scriptures to your life? -

Today's prayers:

Today's passages:

Genesis 23:1-24:51

Matthew 8:1-17

Psalms 9:13-20

Proverbs 3:1-6

Notes

All Access Pass — Day 11

Today's passages:

Genesis 24:52-26:16

Matthew 8:18-34

Psalms 10:1-15

Proverbs 3:7-8

Notes

What verse spoke to you in this reading?

Do the New Testament and Old Testament passages have any similarities?

What other verses come to mind as you read these passages?

What questions do you still have? What do you want to know more about? What lesson or theme are you picking up on?

How can you apply these scriptures to your life? -

Today's prayers:

All Access Pass — Day 12

What verse spoke to you in this reading?

Do the New Testament and Old Testament passages have any similarities?

What other verses come to mind as you read these passages?

What questions do you still have? What do you want to know more about? What lesson or theme are you picking up on?

How can you apply these scriptures to your life? -

Today's prayers:

Today's passages:

Genesis 26:17-27:46

Matthew 9:1-17

Psalms 10:16-18

Proverbs 3:9-10

Notes

All Access Pass — Day 13

Today's passages:

Genesis 28:1-29:35

Matthew 9:18-38

Psalms 11:1-7

Proverbs 3:11-12

What verse spoke to you in this reading?

Do the New Testament and Old Testament passages have any similarities?

What other verses come to mind as you read these passages?

What questions do you still have? What do you want to know more about? What lesson or theme are you picking up on?

How can you apply these scriptures to your life? -

Today's prayers:

All Access Pass — Day 14

Today's passages:

Genesis 30:1-31:16

Matthew 10:1-23

Psalms 12:1-8

Proverbs 3:13-15

What verse spoke to you in this reading?

Do the New Testament and Old Testament passages have any similarities?

What other verses come to mind as you read these passages?

What questions do you still have? What do you want to know more about? What lesson or theme are you picking up on?

How can you apply these scriptures to your life? -

Today's prayers:

All Access Pass — Day 15

Today's passages:

Genesis 31:17-32:12

Matthew 10:24-11:6

Psalms 13:1-6

Proverbs 3:16-18

What verse spoke to you in this reading?

Do the New Testament and Old Testament passages have any similarities?

What other verses come to mind as you read these passages?

What questions do you still have? What do you want to know more about? What lesson or theme are you picking up on?

How can you apply these scriptures to your life? -

Today's prayers:

All Access Pass

Today's passages:

Genesis 32:13-34:31

Matthew 11:7-30

Psalms 14:1-7

Proverbs 3:19-20

What verse spoke to you in this reading?
___

Do the New Testament and Old Testament passages have any similarities?
___

What other verses come to mind as you read these passages?
___

What questions do you still have? What do you want to know more about? What lesson or theme are you picking up on?
___

How can you apply these scriptures to your life? -
___

Today's prayers:
___

All Access Pass

Today's passages:

Genesis 35:1-36:43

Matthew 12:1-21

Psalms 15:1-5

Proverbs 3:21-26

What verse spoke to you in this reading?

Do the New Testament and Old Testament passages have any similarities?

What other verses come to mind as you read these passages?

What questions do you still have? What do you want to know more about? What lesson or theme are you picking up on?

How can you apply these scriptures to your life? -

Today's prayers:

All Access Pass — Day 18

Today's passages:

Genesis 37:1-38:30

Matthew 12:22-45

Psalms 16:1-11

Proverbs 3:27-32

Notes

What verse spoke to you in this reading?

Do the New Testament and Old Testament passages have any similarities?

What other verses come to mind as you read these passages?

What questions do you still have? What do you want to know more about? What lesson or theme are you picking up on?

How can you apply these scriptures to your life? -

Today's prayers:

All Access Pass — Day 19

Today's passages:

Genesis 39:1-41:16

Matthew 12:46-13:23

Psalms 17:1-15

Proverbs 3:33-35

Notes

What verse spoke to you in this reading?

Do the New Testament and Old Testament passages have any similarities?

What other verses come to mind as you read these passages?

What questions do you still have? What do you want to know more about? What lesson or theme are you picking up on?

How can you apply these scriptures to your life? -

Today's prayers:

All Access Pass — Day 20

Today's passages:

Genesis 41:17-42:17

Matthew 13:24-46

Psalms 18:1-15

Proverbs 4:1-6

Notes

What verse spoke to you in this reading?

Do the New Testament and Old Testament passages have any similarities?

What other verses come to mind as you read these passages?

What questions do you still have? What do you want to know more about? What lesson or theme are you picking up on?

How can you apply these scriptures to your life? -

Today's prayers:

All Access Pass — Day 21

Today's passages:

Genesis 42:18-43:34

Matthew 13:47-14:12

Psalms 18:16-36

Proverbs 4:7-10

What verse spoke to you in this reading?

Do the New Testament and Old Testament passages have any similarities?

What other verses come to mind as you read these passages?

What questions do you still have? What do you want to know more about? What lesson or theme are you picking up on?

How can you apply these scriptures to your life? -

Today's prayers:

All Access Pass — Day 22

What verse spoke to you in this reading?

Do the New Testament and Old Testament passages have any similarities?

What other verses come to mind as you read these passages?

What questions do you still have? What do you want to know more about? What lesson or theme are you picking up on?

How can you apply these scriptures to your life? -

Today's prayers:

Today's passages:

Genesis 44:1-45:28

Matthew 14:13-36

Psalms 18:37-50

Proverbs 4:11-13

Notes

All Access Pass — Day 23

Today's passages:

Genesis 46:1-47:31

Matthew 15:1-28

Psalms 19:1-14

Proverbs 4:14-19

What verse spoke to you in this reading?

Do the New Testament and Old Testament passages have any similarities?

What other verses come to mind as you read these passages?

What questions do you still have? What do you want to know more about? What lesson or theme are you picking up on?

How can you apply these scriptures to your life? -

Today's prayers:

All Access Pass — Day 24

What verse spoke to you in this reading?

Do the New Testament and Old Testament passages have any similarities?

What other verses come to mind as you read these passages?

What questions do you still have? What do you want to know more about? What lesson or theme are you picking up on?

How can you apply these scriptures to your life? -

Today's prayers:

Today's passages:

Genesis 48:1-49:33

Matthew 15:29-16:12

Psalms 20:1-9

Proverbs 4:20-27

Notes

All Access Pass — Day 25

Today's passages:

Genesis 50:1-Exodus 2:10

Matthew 16:13-17:9

Psalms 21:1-13

Proverbs 5:1-6

What verse spoke to you in this reading?

Do the New Testament and Old Testament passages have any similarities?

What other verses come to mind as you read these passages?

What questions do you still have? What do you want to know more about? What lesson or theme are you picking up on?

How can you apply these scriptures to your life? -

Today's prayers:

All Access Pass — Day 26

Today's passages:

Exodus 2:11-3:22

Matthew 17:10-27

Psalms 22:1-18

Proverbs 5:7-14

Notes

What verse spoke to you in this reading?

Do the New Testament and Old Testament passages have any similarities?

What other verses come to mind as you read these passages?

What questions do you still have? What do you want to know more about? What lesson or theme are you picking up on?

How can you apply these scriptures to your life? -

Today's prayers:

All Access Pass — Day 27

Today's passages:

Exodus 4:1-5:21

Matthew 18:1-20

Psalms 22:19-31

Proverbs 5:15-21

What verse spoke to you in this reading?

Do the New Testament and Old Testament passages have any similarities?

What other verses come to mind as you read these passages?

What questions do you still have? What do you want to know more about? What lesson or theme are you picking up on?

How can you apply these scriptures to your life? -

Today's prayers:

All Access Pass — Day 28

What verse spoke to you in this reading?
_____
_____
_____

Do the New Testament and Old Testament passages have any similarities?
_____
_____
_____

What other verses come to mind as you read these passages?
_____
_____
_____

What questions do you still have? What do you want to know more about? What lesson or theme are you picking up on?
_____
_____
_____
_____
_____

How can you apply these scriptures to your life? -
_____
_____
_____
_____

Today's prayers:
_____
_____
_____
_____

Today's passages:

Exodus 5:22-7:25

Matthew 18:21-19:12

Psalms 23:1-6

Proverbs 5:22-23

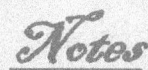

All Access Pass — Day 29

Today's passages:

Exodus 8:1-9:35

Matthew 19:13-30

Psalms 24:1-10

Proverbs 6:1-5

What verse spoke to you in this reading?

Do the New Testament and Old Testament passages have any similarities?

What other verses come to mind as you read these passages?

What questions do you still have? What do you want to know more about? What lesson or theme are you picking up on?

How can you apply these scriptures to your life? -

Today's prayers:

All Access Pass — Day 30

What verse spoke to you in this reading?

Do the New Testament and Old Testament passages have any similarities?

What other verses come to mind as you read these passages?

What questions do you still have? What do you want to know more about? What lesson or theme are you picking up on?

How can you apply these scriptures to your life? -

Today's prayers:

Today's passages:

Exodus 10:1-12:13

Matthew 20:1-28

Psalms 25:1-15

Proverbs 6:6-11

All Access Pass — Day 31

Today's passages:

Exodus 12:14-13:16

Matthew 20:29-21:22

Psalms 25:16-22

Proverbs 6:12-15

Notes

What verse spoke to you in this reading?

Do the New Testament and Old Testament passages have any similarities?

What other verses come to mind as you read these passages?

What questions do you still have? What do you want to know more about? What lesson or theme are you picking up on?

How can you apply these scriptures to your life? -

Today's prayers:

All Access Pass

Today's passages:

Exodus 13:17-15:18

Matthew 21:23-46

Psalms 26:1-12

Proverbs 6:16-19

What verse spoke to you in this reading?

Do the New Testament and Old Testament passages have any similarities?

What other verses come to mind as you read these passages?

What questions do you still have? What do you want to know more about? What lesson or theme are you picking up on?

How can you apply these scriptures to your life? -

Today's prayers:

All Access Pass

Today's passages:

Exodus 15:19-17:7

Matthew 22:1-33

Psalms 27:1-6

Proverbs 6:20-25

What verse spoke to you in this reading?

Do the New Testament and Old Testament passages have any similarities?

What other verses come to mind as you read these passages?

What questions do you still have? What do you want to know more about? What lesson or theme are you picking up on?

How can you apply these scriptures to your life? -

Today's prayers:

All Access Pass — Day 34

What verse spoke to you in this reading?
_____
_____
_____

Do the New Testament and Old Testament passages have any similarities?
_____
_____
_____

What other verses come to mind as you read these passages?
_____
_____
_____

What questions do you still have? What do you want to know more about? What lesson or theme are you picking up on?
_____
_____
_____
_____
_____
_____

How can you apply these scriptures to your life? -
_____
_____
_____
_____

Today's prayers:
_____
_____
_____
_____

Today's passages:

Exodus 17:8-19:15

Matthew 22:34-23:12

Psalms 27:7-14

Proverbs 6:27-35

All Access Pass — Day 35

Today's passages:

Exodus 19:16-21:21

Matthew 23:13-39

Psalms 28:1-9

Proverbs 7:1-5

Notes

What verse spoke to you in this reading?

Do the New Testament and Old Testament passages have any similarities?

What other verses come to mind as you read these passages?

What questions do you still have? What do you want to know more about? What lesson or theme are you picking up on?

How can you apply these scriptures to your life? -

Today's prayers:

All Access Pass — Day 36

Today's passages:

Exodus 21:22-23:13

Matthew 24:1-28

Psalms 29:1-11

Proverbs 7:6-23

Notes

What verse spoke to you in this reading?

Do the New Testament and Old Testament passages have any similarities?

What other verses come to mind as you read these passages?

What questions do you still have? What do you want to know more about? What lesson or theme are you picking up on?

How can you apply these scriptures to your life? -

Today's prayers:

All Access Pass — Day 37

Today's passages:

Exodus 23:14-25:40

Matthew 24:29-51

Psalms 30:1-12

Proverbs 7:24-27

What verse spoke to you in this reading?

Do the New Testament and Old Testament passages have any similarities?

What other verses come to mind as you read these passages?

What questions do you still have? What do you want to know more about? What lesson or theme are you picking up on?

How can you apply these scriptures to your life? -

Today's prayers:

All Access Pass — Day 38

What verse spoke to you in this reading?

Do the New Testament and Old Testament passages have any similarities?

What other verses come to mind as you read these passages?

What questions do you still have? What do you want to know more about? What lesson or theme are you picking up on?

How can you apply these scriptures to your life? -

Today's prayers:

Today's passages:

Exodus 26:1-27:21

Matthew 25:1-30

Psalms 31:1-8

Proverbs 8:1-11

Notes

All Access Pass — Day 39

Today's passages:

Exodus 28:1-43

Matthew 25:31-26:13

Psalms 31:9-18

Proverbs 8:12-13

Notes

What verse spoke to you in this reading?

Do the New Testament and Old Testament passages have any similarities?

What other verses come to mind as you read these passages?

What questions do you still have? What do you want to know more about? What lesson or theme are you picking up on?

How can you apply these scriptures to your life? -

Today's prayers:

All Access Pass — Day 40

What verse spoke to you in this reading?
_____
_____
_____

Do the New Testament and Old Testament passages have any similarities?
_____
_____
_____

What other verses come to mind as you read these passages?
_____
_____
_____

What questions do you still have? What do you want to know more about? What lesson or theme are you picking up on?
_____
_____
_____
_____
_____
_____

How can you apply these scriptures to your life? -
_____
_____
_____
_____

Today's prayers:
_____
_____
_____
_____

Today's passages:

Exodus 29:1-30:10

Matthew 26:14-46

Psalms 31:19-24

Proverbs 8-14-26

Notes

All Access Pass — Day 41

Today's passages:

Exodus 30:11-31:18

Matthew 26:47-68

Psalms 32:1-11

Proverbs 8:27-32

What verse spoke to you in this reading?

Do the New Testament and Old Testament passages have any similarities?

What other verses come to mind as you read these passages?

What questions do you still have? What do you want to know more about? What lesson or theme are you picking up on?

How can you apply these scriptures to your life? -

Today's prayers:

All Access Pass — Day 42

What verse spoke to you in this reading?
_____
_____
_____

Do the New Testament and Old Testament passages have any similarities?
_____
_____
_____

What other verses come to mind as you read these passages?
_____
_____
_____

What questions do you still have? What do you want to know more about? What lesson or theme are you picking up on?
_____
_____
_____
_____
_____

How can you apply these scriptures to your life? -
_____
_____
_____
_____

Today's prayers:
_____
_____
_____
_____

Today's passages:

Exodus 32:1-33:23

Matthew 26:69-27:14

Psalms 33:1-11

Proverbs 8:33-36

All Access Pass — Day 43

Today's passages:

Exodus 34:1-35:9

Matthew 27:15-31

Psalms 33:12-22

Proverbs 9:1-5

Notes

What verse spoke to you in this reading?

Do the New Testament and Old Testament passages have any similarities?

What other verses come to mind as you read these passages?

What questions do you still have? What do you want to know more about? What lesson or theme are you picking up on?

How can you apply these scriptures to your life? -

Today's prayers:

All Access Pass — Day 44

Today's passages:

Exodus 35:10-36:38

Matthew 27:32-66

Psalms 34:1-10

Proverbs 9:7-8

Notes

What verse spoke to you in this reading?

Do the New Testament and Old Testament passages have any similarities?

What other verses come to mind as you read these passages?

What questions do you still have? What do you want to know more about? What lesson or theme are you picking up on?

How can you apply these scriptures to your life? -

Today's prayers:

All Access Pass — Day 45

Today's passages:

Exodus 37:1-38:31

Matthew 28:1-20

Psalms 34:11-22

Proverbs 9:9-10

What verse spoke to you in this reading?

Do the New Testament and Old Testament passages have any similarities?

What other verses come to mind as you read these passages?

What questions do you still have? What do you want to know more about? What lesson or theme are you picking up on?

How can you apply these scriptures to your life? -

Today's prayers:

All Access Pass — Day 46

What verse spoke to you in this reading?

Do the New Testament and Old Testament passages have any similarities?

What other verses come to mind as you read these passages?

What questions do you still have? What do you want to know more about? What lesson or theme are you picking up on?

How can you apply these scriptures to your life? -

Today's prayers:

Today's passages:

Exodus 39:1-40:38

Mark 1:1-28

Psalms 35:1-16

Proverbs 9:11-12

Notes

All Access Pass — Day 47

Today's passages:

Leviticus 1:1-3:17

Mark 1:29-2:12

Psalms 35:17-28

Proverbs 9:13-18

Notes

What verse spoke to you in this reading?

Do the New Testament and Old Testament passages have any similarities?

What other verses come to mind as you read these passages?

What questions do you still have? What do you want to know more about? What lesson or theme are you picking up on?

How can you apply these scriptures to your life? -

Today's prayers:

All Access Pass — Day 48

What verse spoke to you in this reading?

Do the New Testament and Old Testament passages have any similarities?

What other verses come to mind as you read these passages?

What questions do you still have? What do you want to know more about? What lesson or theme are you picking up on?

How can you apply these scriptures to your life? -

Today's prayers:

Today's passages:

Leviticus 4:1-5:19

Mark 2:13-3:6

Psalms 36:1-12

Proverbs 10:1-2

Notes

All Access Pass — Day 49

Today's passages:

Leviticus 6:1-7:27

Mark 3:7-30

Psalms 37:1-11

Proverbs 10:3-4

Notes

What verse spoke to you in this reading?

Do the New Testament and Old Testament passages have any similarities?

What other verses come to mind as you read these passages?

What questions do you still have? What do you want to know more about? What lesson or theme are you picking up on?

How can you apply these scriptures to your life? -

Today's prayers:

All Access Pass — Day 50

What verse spoke to you in this reading?

Do the New Testament and Old Testament passages have any similarities?

What other verses come to mind as you read these passages?

What questions do you still have? What do you want to know more about? What lesson or theme are you picking up on?

How can you apply these scriptures to your life? -

Today's prayers:

Today's passages:

Leviticus 7:28-9:6

Mark 3:31-4:25

Psalm 37:12-29

Proverbs 10:5

Notes

All Access Pass  Day 51

Today's passages:

Leviticus 9:7-10:20

Mark 4:26-5:20

Psalms 37:30-40

Proverbs 10:6-7

What verse spoke to you in this reading?

Do the New Testament and Old Testament passages have any similarities?

What other verses come to mind as you read these passages?

What questions do you still have? What do you want to know more about? What lesson or theme are you picking up on?

How can you apply these scriptures to your life? -

Today's prayers:

All Access Pass — Day 52

Today's passages:

Leviticus 11:1-12:8

Mark 5:21-43

Psalms 38:1-22

Proverbs 10:8-9

Notes

What verse spoke to you in this reading?

Do the New Testament and Old Testament passages have any similarities?

What other verses come to mind as you read these passages?

What questions do you still have? What do you want to know more about? What lesson or theme are you picking up on?

How can you apply these scriptures to your life? -

Today's prayers:

All Access Pass — Day 53

Today's passages:

Leviticus 13:1-59

Mark 6:1-29

Psalms 39:1-13

Proverbs 10:10

What verse spoke to you in this reading?

Do the New Testament and Old Testament passages have any similarities?

What other verses come to mind as you read these passages?

What questions do you still have? What do you want to know more about? What lesson or theme are you picking up on?

How can you apply these scriptures to your life? -

Today's prayers:

All Access Pass — Day 54

Today's passages:

Leviticus 14:1-57

Mark 6:30-56

Psalms 40:1-10

Proverbs 10:11-12

Notes

What verse spoke to you in this reading?

Do the New Testament and Old Testament passages have any similarities?

What other verses come to mind as you read these passages?

What questions do you still have? What do you want to know more about? What lesson or theme are you picking up on?

How can you apply these scriptures to your life? -

Today's prayers:

All Access Pass — Day 55

Today's passages:

Leviticus 15:1-16:28

Mark 7:1-23

Psalms 40:11-17

Proverbs 10:13-14

Notes

What verse spoke to you in this reading?

Do the New Testament and Old Testament passages have any similarities?

What other verses come to mind as you read these passages?

What questions do you still have? What do you want to know more about? What lesson or theme are you picking up on?

How can you apply these scriptures to your life? -

Today's prayers:

# All Access Pass — Day 56

What verse spoke to you in this reading?

Do the New Testament and Old Testament passages have any similarities?

What other verses come to mind as you read these passages?

What questions do you still have? What do you want to know more about? What lesson or theme are you picking up on?

How can you apply these scriptures to your life? -

Today's prayers:

Today's passages:

Leviticus 16:29-18:30

Mark 7:24-8:10

Psalms 41:1-13

Proverbs 10:15-16

Notes

All Access Pass — Day 57

Today's passages:

Leviticus 19:1-20:21

Mark 8:11-38

Psalms 42:1-11

Proverbs 10:17

What verse spoke to you in this reading?

Do the New Testament and Old Testament passages have any similarities?

What other verses come to mind as you read these passages?

What questions do you still have? What do you want to know more about? What lesson or theme are you picking up on?

How can you apply these scriptures to your life? -

Today's prayers:

All Access Pass — Day 58

Today's passages:

Leviticus 20:22-22:16

Mark 9:1-29

Psalms 43:1-5

Proverbs 10:18

What verse spoke to you in this reading?

Do the New Testament and Old Testament passages have any similarities?

What other verses come to mind as you read these passages?

What questions do you still have? What do you want to know more about? What lesson or theme are you picking up on?

How can you apply these scriptures to your life? -

Today's prayers:

All Access Pass — Day 59

Today's passages:

Leviticus 22:17-23:44

Mark 9:30-10:12

Psalm 44:1-8

Proverbs 10:19

Notes

What verse spoke to you in this reading?

Do the New Testament and Old Testament passages have any similarities?

What other verses come to mind as you read these passages?

What questions do you still have? What do you want to know more about? What lesson or theme are you picking up on?

How can you apply these scriptures to your life? -

Today's prayers:

All Access Pass — Day 60

Today's passages:

Leviticus 24:1-25:46

Mark 10:13-31

Psalms 44:9-26

Proverbs 10:20-21

Notes

What verse spoke to you in this reading?

Do the New Testament and Old Testament passages have any similarities?

What other verses come to mind as you read these passages?

What questions do you still have? What do you want to know more about? What lesson or theme are you picking up on?

How can you apply these scriptures to your life? -

Today's prayers:

All Access Pass — Day 61

Today's passages:

Leviticus 25:47-27:13

Mark 10:32-52

Psalms 45:1-17

Proverbs 10:22

What verse spoke to you in this reading?

Do the New Testament and Old Testament passages have any similarities?

What other verses come to mind as you read these passages?

What questions do you still have? What do you want to know more about? What lesson or theme are you picking up on?

How can you apply these scriptures to your life? -

Today's prayers:

All Access Pass — Day 62

What verse spoke to you in this reading?
_____
_____
_____

Do the New Testament and Old Testament passages have any similarities?
_____
_____
_____

What other verses come to mind as you read these passages?
_____
_____
_____

What questions do you still have? What do you want to know more about? What lesson or theme are you picking up on?
_____
_____
_____
_____
_____

How can you apply these scriptures to your life? -
_____
_____
_____
_____
_____

Today's prayers:
_____
_____
_____
_____

Today's passages:

Leviticus 27:14- Numbers 1:54

Mark 11:1-26

Psalms 46:1-11

Proverbs 10:23

Notes

All Access Pass — Day 63

Today's passages:

Numbers 2:1-3:51

Mark 11:27-12:17

Psalms 47:1-9

Proverbs 10:24-25

Notes

What verse spoke to you in this reading?

Do the New Testament and Old Testament passages have any similarities?

What other verses come to mind as you read these passages?

What questions do you still have? What do you want to know more about? What lesson or theme are you picking up on?

How can you apply these scriptures to your life? -

Today's prayers:

All Access Pass — Day 64

What verse spoke to you in this reading?

Do the New Testament and Old Testament passages have any similarities?

What other verses come to mind as you read these passages?

What questions do you still have? What do you want to know more about? What lesson or theme are you picking up on?

How can you apply these scriptures to your life? -

Today's prayers:

Today's passages:

Numbers 4:1-5:31

Mark 12:18-37

Psalms 48:1-14

Proverbs 10:26

Notes

All Access Pass — Day 65

Today's passages:

Numbers 6:1-7:89

Mark 12:38-13:13

Psalms 49:1-20

Proverbs 10:27-28

Notes

What verse spoke to you in this reading?

Do the New Testament and Old Testament passages have any similarities?

What other verses come to mind as you read these passages?

What questions do you still have? What do you want to know more about? What lesson or theme are you picking up on?

How can you apply these scriptures to your life? -

Today's prayers:

All Access Pass — Day 66

What verse spoke to you in this reading?

Do the New Testament and Old Testament passages have any similarities?

What other verses come to mind as you read these passages?

What questions do you still have? What do you want to know more about? What lesson or theme are you picking up on?

How can you apply these scriptures to your life? -

Today's prayers:

Today's passages:

Numbers 8:1-9:23

Mark 13:14-37

Psalms 50:1-23

Proverbs 10:29-30

Notes

All Access Pass — Day 67

Today's passages:

Numbers 10:1-11:23

Mark 14:1-21

Psalms 51:1-19

Proverbs 11:1-3

Notes

What verse spoke to you in this reading?

Do the New Testament and Old Testament passages have any similarities?

What other verses come to mind as you read these passages?

What questions do you still have? What do you want to know more about? What lesson or theme are you picking up on?

How can you apply these scriptures to your life? -

Today's prayers:

All Access Pass — Day 68

Today's passages:

Numbers 11:24-13:33

Mark 14:22-52

Psalms 52:1-9

Proverbs 11:1-3

Notes

What verse spoke to you in this reading?

Do the New Testament and Old Testament passages have any similarities?

What other verses come to mind as you read these passages?

What questions do you still have? What do you want to know more about? What lesson or theme are you picking up on?

How can you apply these scriptures to your life? -

Today's prayers:

All Access Pass — Day 69

Today's passages:

Numbers 14:1-15:16

Mark 14:53-72

Psalms 53:1-6

Proverbs 11:4

Notes

What verse spoke to you in this reading?

Do the New Testament and Old Testament passages have any similarities?

What other verses come to mind as you read these passages?

What questions do you still have? What do you want to know more about? What lesson or theme are you picking up on?

How can you apply these scriptures to your life? -

Today's prayers:

All Access Pass — Day 70

Today's passages:

Numbers 15:17-16:40

Mark 15:1-47

Psalms 54:1-7

Proverbs 11:5-6

Notes

What verse spoke to you in this reading?

Do the New Testament and Old Testament passages have any similarities?

What other verses come to mind as you read these passages?

What questions do you still have? What do you want to know more about? What lesson or theme are you picking up on?

How can you apply these scriptures to your life? -

Today's prayers:

All Access Pass — Day 71

Today's passages:

Numbers 16:41-18:32

Mark 16:1-20

Psalms 55:1-23

Proverbs 11:7

Notes

What verse spoke to you in this reading?

Do the New Testament and Old Testament passages have any similarities?

What other verses come to mind as you read these passages?

What questions do you still have? What do you want to know more about? What lesson or theme are you picking up on?

How can you apply these scriptures to your life? -

Today's prayers:

All Access Pass — Day 72

Today's passages:

Numbers 19:1-20:29

Luke 1:1-25

Psalms 56:1-13

Proverbs 11:8

Notes

What verse spoke to you in this reading?

Do the New Testament and Old Testament passages have any similarities?

What other verses come to mind as you read these passages?

What questions do you still have? What do you want to know more about? What lesson or theme are you picking up on?

How can you apply these scriptures to your life? -

Today's prayers:

All Access Pass — Day 73

Today's passages:

Numbers 21:1-22:20

Luke 1:26-56

Psalms 57:1-11

Proverbs 11:9-11

Notes

What verse spoke to you in this reading?

Do the New Testament and Old Testament passages have any similarities?

What other verses come to mind as you read these passages?

What questions do you still have? What do you want to know more about? What lesson or theme are you picking up on?

How can you apply these scriptures to your life? -

Today's prayers:

All Access Pass — Day 74

What verse spoke to you in this reading?
_____
_____
_____

Do the New Testament and Old Testament passages have any similarities?
_____
_____
_____

What other verses come to mind as you read these passages?
_____
_____
_____

What questions do you still have? What do you want to know more about? What lesson or theme are you picking up on?
_____
_____
_____
_____
_____

How can you apply these scriptures to your life? -
_____
_____
_____
_____

Today's prayers:
_____
_____
_____
_____

Today's passages:

Numbers 22:21-23:30

Luke 1:57-80

Psalms 58:1-11

Proverbs 11:12-13

Notes

All Access Pass — Day 75

Today's passages:

Numbers 24:1-25:18

Luke 2:1-35

Psalms 59:1-17

Proverbs 11:14

What verse spoke to you in this reading?

Do the New Testament and Old Testament passages have any similarities?

What other verses come to mind as you read these passages?

What questions do you still have? What do you want to know more about? What lesson or theme are you picking up on?

How can you apply these scriptures to your life? -

Today's prayers:

All Access Pass — Day 76

What verse spoke to you in this reading?
_____
_____
_____

Do the New Testament and Old Testament passages have any similarities?
_____
_____
_____

What other verses come to mind as you read these passages?
_____
_____
_____
_____

What questions do you still have? What do you want to know more about? What lesson or theme are you picking up on?
_____
_____
_____
_____
_____
_____

How can you apply these scriptures to your life? -
_____
_____
_____
_____
_____

Today's prayers:
_____
_____
_____
_____

Today's passages:

Numbers 26:1-51

Luke 2:36-52

Psalms 60:1-12

Proverbs 11:15

Notes

All Access Pass — Day 77

Today's passages:

Numbers 26:52-28:15

Luke 3:1-22

Psalm 61:1-8

Proverbs 11:16-17

Notes

What verse spoke to you in this reading?

Do the New Testament and Old Testament passages have any similarities?

What other verses come to mind as you read these passages?

What questions do you still have? What do you want to know more about? What lesson or theme are you picking up on?

How can you apply these scriptures to your life? -

Today's prayers:

All Access Pass — Day 78

What verse spoke to you in this reading?

Do the New Testament and Old Testament passages have any similarities?

What other verses come to mind as you read these passages?

What questions do you still have? What do you want to know more about? What lesson or theme are you picking up on?

How can you apply these scriptures to your life? -

Today's prayers:

Today's passages:

Numbers 28:16-29:40

Luke 3:23-38

Psalm 62:1-12

Proverbs 11:18-19

Notes

All Access Pass — Day 79

Today's passages:

Numbers 30:1-31:54

Luke 4:1-30

Psalm 63:1-11

Proverbs 11:20-21

What verse spoke to you in this reading?

Do the New Testament and Old Testament passages have any similarities?

What other verses come to mind as you read these passages?

What questions do you still have? What do you want to know more about? What lesson or theme are you picking up on?

How can you apply these scriptures to your life? -

Today's prayers:

All Access Pass — Day 80

Numbers 32:1-33:39

Luke 4:31-5:11

Psalm 64:1-10

Proverbs 11:22

Notes

What verse spoke to you in this reading?

Do the New Testament and Old Testament passages have any similarities?

What other verses come to mind as you read these passages?

What questions do you still have? What do you want to know more about? What lesson or theme are you picking up on?

How can you apply these scriptures to your life? -

Today's prayers:

All Access Pass Day 81

Today's passages:

Numbers 33:40-35:34

Luke 5:12-28

Psalm 65:1-13

Proverbs 11:23

What verse spoke to you in this reading?

Do the New Testament and Old Testament passages have any similarities?

What other verses come to mind as you read these passages?

What questions do you still have? What do you want to know more about? What lesson or theme are you picking up on?

How can you apply these scriptures to your life? -

Today's prayers:

All Access Pass — Day 82

Today's passages:

Numbers 36:1-

Deuteronomy 1:46

Luke 5:29-6:11

Psalm 66:1-20

Proverbs 11:24-26

Notes

What verse spoke to you in this reading?

Do the New Testament and Old Testament passages have any similarities?

What other verses come to mind as you read these passages?

What questions do you still have? What do you want to know more about? What lesson or theme are you picking up on?

How can you apply these scriptures to your life? -

Today's prayers:

All Access Pass — Day 83

Today's passages:

Deuteronomy 2:1-3:29

Luke 6:12-38

Psalm 67:1-7

Proverbs 11:27

Notes

What verse spoke to you in this reading?

Do the New Testament and Old Testament passages have any similarities?

What other verses come to mind as you read these passages?

What questions do you still have? What do you want to know more about? What lesson or theme are you picking up on?

How can you apply these scriptures to your life? -

Today's prayers:

All Access Pass — Day 84

What verse spoke to you in this reading?

Do the New Testament and Old Testament passages have any similarities?

What other verses come to mind as you read these passages?

What questions do you still have? What do you want to know more about? What lesson or theme are you picking up on?

How can you apply these scriptures to your life? -

Today's prayers:

Today's passages:

Deuteronomy 4:1-49

Luke 6:39-7:10

Psalm 68:1-18

Proverbs 11:28

Notes

All Access Pass — Day 85

Today's passages:

Deuteronomy 5:1-6:25

Luke 7:11-35

Psalm 68:19-35

Proverbs 11:29-31

Notes

What verse spoke to you in this reading?

Do the New Testament and Old Testament passages have any similarities?

What other verses come to mind as you read these passages?

What questions do you still have? What do you want to know more about? What lesson or theme are you picking up on?

How can you apply these scriptures to your life? -

Today's prayers:

All Access Pass — Day 86

What verse spoke to you in this reading?
_____
_____
_____

Do the New Testament and Old Testament passages have any similarities?
_____
_____
_____

What other verses come to mind as you read these passages?
_____
_____
_____

What questions do you still have? What do you want to know more about? What lesson or theme are you picking up on?
_____
_____
_____
_____
_____
_____

How can you apply these scriptures to your life? -
_____
_____
_____
_____

Today's prayers:
_____
_____
_____
_____

Today's passages:

Deuteronomy 7:1-8:20

Luke 7:36-8:3

Psalm 69:1-18

Proverbs 12:1

Notes

All Access Pass — Day 87

Today's passages:

Deuteronomy 9:1-10:22

Luke 8:4-21

Psalm 69:19-36

Proverbs 12:2-3

What verse spoke to you in this reading?

Do the New Testament and Old Testament passages have any similarities?

What other verses come to mind as you read these passages?

What questions do you still have? What do you want to know more about? What lesson or theme are you picking up on?

How can you apply these scriptures to your life? -

Today's prayers:

All Access Pass — Day 88

Today's passages:

Deuteronomy 11:1-12:32

Luke 8:22-39

Psalm 70:1-5

Proverbs 12:4

What verse spoke to you in this reading?

Do the New Testament and Old Testament passages have any similarities?

What other verses come to mind as you read these passages?

What questions do you still have? What do you want to know more about? What lesson or theme are you picking up on?

How can you apply these scriptures to your life? -

Today's prayers:

All Access Pass — Day 89

Today's passages:

Deuteronomy 13:1-15:23

Luke 8:40-9:6

Psalm 71:1-24

Proverbs 12:5-7

Notes

What verse spoke to you in this reading?

Do the New Testament and Old Testament passages have any similarities?

What other verses come to mind as you read these passages?

What questions do you still have? What do you want to know more about? What lesson or theme are you picking up on?

How can you apply these scriptures to your life? -

Today's prayers:

All Access Pass — Day 90

Today's passages:

Deuteronomy 16:1-17:20

Luke 9:7-27

Psalm 72:1-20

Proverbs 12:8-9

What verse spoke to you in this reading?

Do the New Testament and Old Testament passages have any similarities?

What other verses come to mind as you read these passages?

What questions do you still have? What do you want to know more about? What lesson or theme are you picking up on?

How can you apply these scriptures to your life? -

Today's prayers:

All Access Pass — Day 91

Today's passages:

Deuteronomy 18:1-20:20

Luke 9:28-50

Psalm 73:1-28

Proverbs 12:10

What verse spoke to you in this reading?

Do the New Testament and Old Testament passages have any similarities?

What other verses come to mind as you read these passages?

What questions do you still have? What do you want to know more about? What lesson or theme are you picking up on?

How can you apply these scriptures to your life? -

Today's prayers:

All Access Pass — Day 92

What verse spoke to you in this reading?

Do the New Testament and Old Testament passages have any similarities?

What other verses come to mind as you read these passages?

What questions do you still have? What do you want to know more about? What lesson or theme are you picking up on?

How can you apply these scriptures to your life? -

Today's prayers:

Today's passages:

Deuteronomy 21:1-22:30

Luke 9:51-10:12

Psalm 74:1-23

Proverbs 12:11

Notes

All Access Pass — Day 93

Today's passages:

Deuteronomy 23:1-25:19

Luke 10:13-37

Psalm 75:1-10

Proverbs 12:12-14

Notes

What verse spoke to you in this reading?

Do the New Testament and Old Testament passages have any similarities?

What other verses come to mind as you read these passages?

What questions do you still have? What do you want to know more about? What lesson or theme are you picking up on?

How can you apply these scriptures to your life? -

Today's prayers:

All Access Pass — Day 94

Today's passages:

Deuteronomy 26:1-27:26

Luke 10:38-11:13

Psalm 76:1-12

Proverbs 12:15-17

Notes

What verse spoke to you in this reading?

Do the New Testament and Old Testament passages have any similarities?

What other verses come to mind as you read these passages?

What questions do you still have? What do you want to know more about? What lesson or theme are you picking up on?

How can you apply these scriptures to your life? -

Today's prayers:

All Access Pass — Day 95

Today's passages:

Deuteronomy 28:1-68

Luke 11:14-36

Psalm 77:1-20

Proverbs 12:18

What verse spoke to you in this reading?

Do the New Testament and Old Testament passages have any similarities?

What other verses come to mind as you read these passages?

What questions do you still have? What do you want to know more about? What lesson or theme are you picking up on?

How can you apply these scriptures to your life? -

Today's prayers:

All Access Pass — Day 96

Today's passages:

Deuteronomy 29:1-30:20

Luke 11:37-12:7

Psalm 78:1-31

Proverbs 12:19-20

Notes

What verse spoke to you in this reading?

Do the New Testament and Old Testament passages have any similarities?

What other verses come to mind as you read these passages?

What questions do you still have? What do you want to know more about? What lesson or theme are you picking up on?

How can you apply these scriptures to your life? -

Today's prayers:

All Access Pass — Day 97

Today's passages:

Deuteronomy 31:1-32:27

Luke 12:8-34

Psalm 78:32-55

Proverbs 12:21-23

Notes

What verse spoke to you in this reading?

Do the New Testament and Old Testament passages have any similarities?

What other verses come to mind as you read these passages?

What questions do you still have? What do you want to know more about? What lesson or theme are you picking up on?

How can you apply these scriptures to your life? -

Today's prayers:

All Access Pass — Day 98

What verse spoke to you in this reading?

Do the New Testament and Old Testament passages have any similarities?

What other verses come to mind as you read these passages?

What questions do you still have? What do you want to know more about? What lesson or theme are you picking up on?

How can you apply these scriptures to your life? -

Today's prayers:

Today's passages:

Deuteronomy 32:28-52

Luke 12:35-59

Psalm 78:56-64

Proverbs 12:24

Notes

All Access Pass — Day 99

Today's passages:

Deuteronomy 33:1-29

Luke 13:1-21

Psalm 78:65-72

Proverbs 12:25

Notes

What verse spoke to you in this reading?

Do the New Testament and Old Testament passages have any similarities?

What other verses come to mind as you read these passages?

What questions do you still have? What do you want to know more about? What lesson or theme are you picking up on?

How can you apply these scriptures to your life? -

Today's prayers:

All Access Pass — Day 100

What verse spoke to you in this reading?

Do the New Testament and Old Testament passages have any similarities?

What other verses come to mind as you read these passages?

What questions do you still have? What do you want to know more about? What lesson or theme are you picking up on?

How can you apply these scriptures to your life? -

Today's prayers:

Today's passages:

Deuteronomy 34:1-

Joshua 2:24

Luke 13:22-14:6

Psalm 79:1-13

Proverbs 12:26

Notes

All Access Pass — Day 101

Today's passages:

Joshua 3:1-4:24

Luke 14:7-35

Psalm 80:1-19

Proverbs 12:27-28

Notes

What verse spoke to you in this reading?

Do the New Testament and Old Testament passages have any similarities?

What other verses come to mind as you read these passages?

What questions do you still have? What do you want to know more about? What lesson or theme are you picking up on?

How can you apply these scriptures to your life? -

Today's prayers:

All Access Pass — Day 102

Today's passages:

Joshua 5:1-7:15

Luke 15:1-32

Psalm 81:1-16

Proverbs 13:1

Notes

What verse spoke to you in this reading?

Do the New Testament and Old Testament passages have any similarities?

What other verses come to mind as you read these passages?

What questions do you still have? What do you want to know more about? What lesson or theme are you picking up on?

How can you apply these scriptures to your life? -

Today's prayers:

All Access Pass — Day 103

Today's passages:

Joshua 7:16-9:2

Luke 16:1-18

Psalm 82:1-8

Proverbs 13:2-3

Notes

What verse spoke to you in this reading?

Do the New Testament and Old Testament passages have any similarities?

What other verses come to mind as you read these passages?

What questions do you still have? What do you want to know more about? What lesson or theme are you picking up on?

How can you apply these scriptures to your life? -

Today's prayers:

All Access Pass — Day 104

Today's passages:

Joshua 9:3-10:43

Luke 16:19-17:10

Psalm 83:1-18

Proverbs 13:4

Notes

What verse spoke to you in this reading?

Do the New Testament and Old Testament passages have any similarities?

What other verses come to mind as you read these passages?

What questions do you still have? What do you want to know more about? What lesson or theme are you picking up on?

How can you apply these scriptures to your life? -

Today's prayers:

All Access Pass — Day 105

Today's passages:

Joshua 11:1-12:24

Luke 17:11-37

Psalm 84:1-12

Proverbs 13:5-6

Notes

What verse spoke to you in this reading?

Do the New Testament and Old Testament passages have any similarities?

What other verses come to mind as you read these passages?

What questions do you still have? What do you want to know more about? What lesson or theme are you picking up on?

How can you apply these scriptures to your life? -

Today's prayers:

All Access Pass — Day 106

Today's passages:

Joshua 13:1-14:15

Luke 18:1-17

Psalm 85:1-13

Proverbs 13:7-8

Notes

What verse spoke to you in this reading?

Do the New Testament and Old Testament passages have any similarities?

What other verses come to mind as you read these passages?

What questions do you still have? What do you want to know more about? What lesson or theme are you picking up on?

How can you apply these scriptures to your life? -

Today's prayers:

All Access Pass — Day 107

Today's passages:

Joshua 15:1-63

Luke 18:18-43

Psalm 86:1-17

Proverbs 13:9-10

What verse spoke to you in this reading?

Do the New Testament and Old Testament passages have any similarities?

What other verses come to mind as you read these passages?

What questions do you still have? What do you want to know more about? What lesson or theme are you picking up on?

How can you apply these scriptures to your life? -

Today's prayers:

All Access Pass — Day 108

Today's passages:

Joshua 16:1-18:28

Luke 19:1-27

Psalm 87:1-7

Proverbs 13:11

Notes

What verse spoke to you in this reading?

Do the New Testament and Old Testament passages have any similarities?

What other verses come to mind as you read these passages?

What questions do you still have? What do you want to know more about? What lesson or theme are you picking up on?

How can you apply these scriptures to your life? -

Today's prayers:

All Access Pass — Day 109

Today's passages:

Joshua 19:1-20:9

Luke 19:28-48

Psalm 88:1-18

Proverbs 13:12-14

Notes

What verse spoke to you in this reading?

Do the New Testament and Old Testament passages have any similarities?

What other verses come to mind as you read these passages?

What questions do you still have? What do you want to know more about? What lesson or theme are you picking up on?

How can you apply these scriptures to your life? -

Today's prayers:

All Access Pass — Day 110

What verse spoke to you in this reading?
___

Do the New Testament and Old Testament passages have any similarities?
___

What other verses come to mind as you read these passages?
___

What questions do you still have? What do you want to know more about? What lesson or theme are you picking up on?
___

How can you apply these scriptures to your life? -
___

Today's prayers:
___

Today's passages:

Joshua 21:1-22:20

Luke 20:1-26

Psalm 89:1-13

Proverbs 13:15-16

Notes

All Access Pass — Day 111

Today's passages:

Joshua 22:21-23:16

Luke 20:27-47

Psalm 89:14-37

Proverbs 13:17-19

What verse spoke to you in this reading?

Do the New Testament and Old Testament passages have any similarities?

What other verses come to mind as you read these passages?

What questions do you still have? What do you want to know more about? What lesson or theme are you picking up on?

How can you apply these scriptures to your life? -

Today's prayers:

All Access Pass — Day 112

What verse spoke to you in this reading?
_____
_____
_____

Do the New Testament and Old Testament passages have any similarities?
_____
_____
_____

What other verses come to mind as you read these passages?
_____
_____
_____

What questions do you still have? What do you want to know more about? What lesson or theme are you picking up on?
_____
_____
_____
_____
_____
_____

How can you apply these scriptures to your life? -
_____
_____
_____
_____

Today's prayers:
_____
_____
_____
_____

Today's passages:

Joshua 24:1-33

Luke 21:1-28

Psalm 89:38-52

Proverbs 13:20-23

Notes

All Access Pass — Day 113

Today's passages:

Judges 1:1-2:9

Luke 21:29-22:13

Psalm 90:1-91:16

Proverbs 13:24-25

What verse spoke to you in this reading?

Do the New Testament and Old Testament passages have any similarities?

What other verses come to mind as you read these passages?

What questions do you still have? What do you want to know more about? What lesson or theme are you picking up on?

How can you apply these scriptures to your life? -

Today's prayers:

All Access Pass — Day 114

Today's passages:

Judges 2:10-3:31

Luke 22:14-34

Psalm 92:1-93:5

Proverbs 14:1-2

Notes

What verse spoke to you in this reading?

Do the New Testament and Old Testament passages have any similarities?

What other verses come to mind as you read these passages?

What questions do you still have? What do you want to know more about? What lesson or theme are you picking up on?

How can you apply these scriptures to your life? -

Today's prayers:

All Access Pass — Day 115

Today's passages:

Judges 4:1-5:31

Luke 22:35-53

Psalm 94:1-23

Proverbs 14:3-4

Notes

What verse spoke to you in this reading?

Do the New Testament and Old Testament passages have any similarities?

What other verses come to mind as you read these passages?

What questions do you still have? What do you want to know more about? What lesson or theme are you picking up on?

How can you apply these scriptures to your life? -

Today's prayers:

All Access Pass — Day 116

Today's passages:

Judges 6:1-40

Luke 22:54-23:12

Psalm 95:1-96:13

Proverbs 14:5-6

Notes

What verse spoke to you in this reading?

Do the New Testament and Old Testament passages have any similarities?

What other verses come to mind as you read these passages?

What questions do you still have? What do you want to know more about? What lesson or theme are you picking up on?

How can you apply these scriptures to your life? -

Today's prayers:

All Access Pass — Day 117

Today's passages:

Judges 7:1-8:17

Luke 23:13-43

Psalm 97:1-98:9

Proverbs 14:7-8

Notes

What verse spoke to you in this reading?

Do the New Testament and Old Testament passages have any similarities?

What other verses come to mind as you read these passages?

What questions do you still have? What do you want to know more about? What lesson or theme are you picking up on?

How can you apply these scriptures to your life? -

Today's prayers:

All Access Pass — Day 118

Today's passages:

Judges 8:18-9:21

Luke 23:44-24:12

Psalm 99:1-9

Proverbs 14:9-10

Notes

What verse spoke to you in this reading?

Do the New Testament and Old Testament passages have any similarities?

What other verses come to mind as you read these passages?

What questions do you still have? What do you want to know more about? What lesson or theme are you picking up on?

How can you apply these scriptures to your life? -

Today's prayers:

All Access Pass — Day 119

Today's passages:

Judges 9:22-10:18

Luke 24:13-53

Psalm 100:1-5

Proverbs 14:11-12

Notes

What verse spoke to you in this reading?

Do the New Testament and Old Testament passages have any similarities?

What other verses come to mind as you read these passages?

What questions do you still have? What do you want to know more about? What lesson or theme are you picking up on?

How can you apply these scriptures to your life? -

Today's prayers:

All Access Pass — Day 120

Today's passages:

Judges 11:1-12:15

John 1:1-28

Psalm 101:1-8

Proverbs 14:13-14

Notes

What verse spoke to you in this reading?

Do the New Testament and Old Testament passages have any similarities?

What other verses come to mind as you read these passages?

What questions do you still have? What do you want to know more about? What lesson or theme are you picking up on?

How can you apply these scriptures to your life? -

Today's prayers:

All Access Pass — Day 121

Today's passages:

Judges 13:1-14:20

John 1:29-51

Psalm 102:1-28

Proverbs 14:15-16

Notes

What verse spoke to you in this reading?

Do the New Testament and Old Testament passages have any similarities?

What other verses come to mind as you read these passages?

What questions do you still have? What do you want to know more about? What lesson or theme are you picking up on?

How can you apply these scriptures to your life? -

Today's prayers:

All Access Pass — Day 122

What verse spoke to you in this reading?

Do the New Testament and Old Testament passages have any similarities?

What other verses come to mind as you read these passages?

What questions do you still have? What do you want to know more about? What lesson or theme are you picking up on?

How can you apply these scriptures to your life? -

Today's prayers:

Today's passages:

Judges 15:1-16:31

John 2:1-25

Psalm 103:1-22

Proverbs 14:17-19

Notes

All Access Pass — Day 123

Today's passages:

Judges 17:1-18:31

John 3:1-21

Psalm 104:1-24

Proverbs 14:20-21

What verse spoke to you in this reading?

Do the New Testament and Old Testament passages have any similarities?

What other verses come to mind as you read these passages?

What questions do you still have? What do you want to know more about? What lesson or theme are you picking up on?

How can you apply these scriptures to your life? -

Today's prayers:

All Access Pass — Day 124

Today's passages:

Judges 19:1-20:48

John 3:22-4:3

Psalm 104:24-35

Proverbs 14:22-23

Notes

What verse spoke to you in this reading?

Do the New Testament and Old Testament passages have any similarities?

What other verses come to mind as you read these passages?

What questions do you still have? What do you want to know more about? What lesson or theme are you picking up on?

How can you apply these scriptures to your life? -

Today's prayers:

All Access Pass — Day 125

Today's passages:

Judges 21:1-Ruth 1:22

John 4:4-42

Psalm 105:1-15

Proverbs 14:25

Notes

What verse spoke to you in this reading?

Do the New Testament and Old Testament passages have any similarities?

What other verses come to mind as you read these passages?

What questions do you still have? What do you want to know more about? What lesson or theme are you picking up on?

How can you apply these scriptures to your life? -

Today's prayers:

All Access Pass — Day 126

Today's passages:

Ruth 2:1-4:22

John 4:43-54

Psalm 105:16-36

Proverbs 14:26-27

Notes

What verse spoke to you in this reading?

Do the New Testament and Old Testament passages have any similarities?

What other verses come to mind as you read these passages?

What questions do you still have? What do you want to know more about? What lesson or theme are you picking up on?

How can you apply these scriptures to your life? -

Today's prayers:

All Access Pass — Day 127

Today's passages:

1 Samuel 1:1-2:21

John 5:1-23

Psalm 105:37-45

Proverbs 14:28-29

Notes

What verse spoke to you in this reading?

Do the New Testament and Old Testament passages have any similarities?

What other verses come to mind as you read these passages?

What questions do you still have? What do you want to know more about? What lesson or theme are you picking up on?

How can you apply these scriptures to your life? -

Today's prayers:

All Access Pass — Day 128

Today's passages:

1 Samuel 2:22-4:22

John 5:24-47

Psalm 106:1-12

Proverbs 14:30-31

Notes

What verse spoke to you in this reading?

Do the New Testament and Old Testament passages have any similarities?

What other verses come to mind as you read these passages?

What questions do you still have? What do you want to know more about? What lesson or theme are you picking up on?

How can you apply these scriptures to your life? -

Today's prayers:

All Access Pass — Day 129

Today's passages:

1 Samuel 5:1-7:17

John 6:1-21

Psalm 106:13-31

Proverbs 14:32-33

Notes

What verse spoke to you in this reading?

Do the New Testament and Old Testament passages have any similarities?

What other verses come to mind as you read these passages?

What questions do you still have? What do you want to know more about? What lesson or theme are you picking up on?

How can you apply these scriptures to your life? -

Today's prayers:

All Access Pass — Day 130

What verse spoke to you in this reading?

Do the New Testament and Old Testament passages have any similarities?

What other verses come to mind as you read these passages?

What questions do you still have? What do you want to know more about? What lesson or theme are you picking up on?

How can you apply these scriptures to your life? -

Today's prayers:

Today's passages:

1 Samuel 8:1-9:27

John 6:22-42

Psalm 106:32-48

Proverbs 14:34-35

Notes

All Access Pass — Day 131

Today's passages:

1 Samuel 10:1-11:15

John 6:43-71

Psalm 107:1-43

Proverbs 15:1-3

Notes

What verse spoke to you in this reading?

Do the New Testament and Old Testament passages have any similarities?

What other verses come to mind as you read these passages?

What questions do you still have? What do you want to know more about? What lesson or theme are you picking up on?

How can you apply these scriptures to your life? -

Today's prayers:

All Access Pass — Day 132

What verse spoke to you in this reading?

Do the New Testament and Old Testament passages have any similarities?

What other verses come to mind as you read these passages?

What questions do you still have? What do you want to know more about? What lesson or theme are you picking up on?

How can you apply these scriptures to your life? -

Today's prayers:

Today's passages:

1 Samuel 12:1-13:23

John 7:1-30

Psalm 108:1-13

Proverbs 15:4

Notes

All Access Pass — Day 133

Today's passages:

1 Samuel 14:1-52

John 7:31-53

Psalm 109:1-31

Proverbs 15:5-7

Notes

What verse spoke to you in this reading?

Do the New Testament and Old Testament passages have any similarities?

What other verses come to mind as you read these passages?

What questions do you still have? What do you want to know more about? What lesson or theme are you picking up on?

How can you apply these scriptures to your life? -

Today's prayers:

All Access Pass — Day 134

Today's passages:

1 Samuel 15:1-16:23

John 8:1-20

Psalm 110:1-7

Proverbs 15:8-10

Notes

What verse spoke to you in this reading?

Do the New Testament and Old Testament passages have any similarities?

What other verses come to mind as you read these passages?

What questions do you still have? What do you want to know more about? What lesson or theme are you picking up on?

How can you apply these scriptures to your life? -

Today's prayers:

All Access Pass — Day 135

Today's passages:

1 Samuel 17:1-18:4

John 8:21-30

Psalm 111:1-10

Proverbs 15:11

Notes

What verse spoke to you in this reading?

Do the New Testament and Old Testament passages have any similarities?

What other verses come to mind as you read these passages?

What questions do you still have? What do you want to know more about? What lesson or theme are you picking up on?

How can you apply these scriptures to your life? -

Today's prayers:

 **Day 136**

What verse spoke to you in this reading?

Do the New Testament and Old Testament passages have any similarities?

What other verses come to mind as you read these passages?

What questions do you still have? What do you want to know more about? What lesson or theme are you picking up on?

How can you apply these scriptures to your life? -

Today's prayers:

Today's passages:

1 Samuel 18:5-19:24

John 8:31-59

Psalm 112:1-10

Proverbs 15:12-14

All Access Pass — Day 137

Today's passages:

1 Samuel 20:1-21:15

John 9:1-41

Psalm 113:1-114:8

Proverbs 15:15-17

Notes

What verse spoke to you in this reading?

Do the New Testament and Old Testament passages have any similarities?

What other verses come to mind as you read these passages?

What questions do you still have? What do you want to know more about? What lesson or theme are you picking up on?

How can you apply these scriptures to your life? -

Today's prayers:

All Access Pass — Day 138

Today's passages:

1 Samuel 22:1-23:29

John 10:1-21

Psalm 115:1-18

Proverbs 15:18-19

Notes

What verse spoke to you in this reading?

Do the New Testament and Old Testament passages have any similarities?

What other verses come to mind as you read these passages?

What questions do you still have? What do you want to know more about? What lesson or theme are you picking up on?

How can you apply these scriptures to your life? -

Today's prayers:

All Access Pass — Day 139

Today's passages:

1 Samuel 24:1-25:44

John 10:22-42

Psalm 116:1-19

Proverbs 15:20-21

Notes

What verse spoke to you in this reading?

Do the New Testament and Old Testament passages have any similarities?

What other verses come to mind as you read these passages?

What questions do you still have? What do you want to know more about? What lesson or theme are you picking up on?

How can you apply these scriptures to your life? -

Today's prayers:

All Access Pass — Day 140

What verse spoke to you in this reading?
_____
_____
_____

Do the New Testament and Old Testament passages have any similarities?
_____
_____
_____

What other verses come to mind as you read these passages?
_____
_____
_____
_____

What questions do you still have? What do you want to know more about? What lesson or theme are you picking up on?
_____
_____
_____
_____
_____
_____

How can you apply these scriptures to your life? -
_____
_____
_____
_____

Today's prayers:
_____
_____
_____
_____

Today's passages:

1 Samuel 26:1-28:25

John 11:1-54

Psalm 117:1-2

Proverbs 15:22-23

Notes

All Access Pass — Day 141

Today's passages:

1 Samuel 29:1-31:13

John 11:55-12:19

Psalm 118:1-18

Proverbs 15:24-26

What verse spoke to you in this reading?

Do the New Testament and Old Testament passages have any similarities?

What other verses come to mind as you read these passages?

What questions do you still have? What do you want to know more about? What lesson or theme are you picking up on?

How can you apply these scriptures to your life? -

Today's prayers:

All Access Pass — Day 142

Today's passages:

2 Samuel 1:1-2:11

John 12:20-50

Psalm 118:19-29

Proverbs 15:27-28

Notes

What verse spoke to you in this reading?

Do the New Testament and Old Testament passages have any similarities?

What other verses come to mind as you read these passages?

What questions do you still have? What do you want to know more about? What lesson or theme are you picking up on?

How can you apply these scriptures to your life? -

Today's prayers:

All Access Pass — Day 143

Today's passages:

2 Samuel 2:12-3:39

John 13:1-30

Psalm 119:1-16

Proverbs 15:29-30

What verse spoke to you in this reading?

Do the New Testament and Old Testament passages have any similarities?

What other verses come to mind as you read these passages?

What questions do you still have? What do you want to know more about? What lesson or theme are you picking up on?

How can you apply these scriptures to your life? -

Today's prayers:

All Access Pass — Day 144

Today's passages:

2 Samuel 4:1-6:23

John 13:31-14:14

Psalm 119:17-32

Proverbs 15:31-32

Notes

What verse spoke to you in this reading?

Do the New Testament and Old Testament passages have any similarities?

What other verses come to mind as you read these passages?

What questions do you still have? What do you want to know more about? What lesson or theme are you picking up on?

How can you apply these scriptures to your life? -

Today's prayers:

All Access Pass — Day 145

Today's passages:

2 Samuel 7:1-8:18

John 14:15-31

Psalm 119:33-48

Proverbs 15:33

Notes

What verse spoke to you in this reading?

Do the New Testament and Old Testament passages have any similarities?

What other verses come to mind as you read these passages?

What questions do you still have? What do you want to know more about? What lesson or theme are you picking up on?

How can you apply these scriptures to your life? -

Today's prayers:

All Access Pass — Day 146

Today's passages:

2 Samuel 9:1-11:27

John 15:1-27

Psalm 119:49-64

Proverbs 16:1-3

Notes

What verse spoke to you in this reading?

Do the New Testament and Old Testament passages have any similarities?

What other verses come to mind as you read these passages?

What questions do you still have? What do you want to know more about? What lesson or theme are you picking up on?

How can you apply these scriptures to your life? -

Today's prayers:

All Access Pass — Day 147

Today's passages:

2 Samuel 12:1-31

John 16:1-33

Psalm 119:65-80

Proverbs 16:4-5

Notes

What verse spoke to you in this reading?

Do the New Testament and Old Testament passages have any similarities?

What other verses come to mind as you read these passages?

What questions do you still have? What do you want to know more about? What lesson or theme are you picking up on?

How can you apply these scriptures to your life? -

Today's prayers:

 **Day 148**

Today's passages:

2 Samuel 13:1-39

John 17:1-26

Psalm 119:81-96

Proverbs 16:6-7

What verse spoke to you in this reading?

Do the New Testament and Old Testament passages have any similarities?

What other verses come to mind as you read these passages?

What questions do you still have? What do you want to know more about? What lesson or theme are you picking up on?

How can you apply these scriptures to your life? -

Today's prayers:

All Access Pass — Day 149

Today's passages:

2 Samuel 14:1-15:22

John 18:1-24

Psalm 119:97-112

Proverbs 16:8-9

Notes

What verse spoke to you in this reading?

Do the New Testament and Old Testament passages have any similarities?

What other verses come to mind as you read these passages?

What questions do you still have? What do you want to know more about? What lesson or theme are you picking up on?

How can you apply these scriptures to your life? -

Today's prayers:

All Access Pass — Day 150

What verse spoke to you in this reading?

Do the New Testament and Old Testament passages have any similarities?

What other verses come to mind as you read these passages?

What questions do you still have? What do you want to know more about? What lesson or theme are you picking up on?

How can you apply these scriptures to your life? -

Today's prayers:

Today's passages:

2 Samuel 15:23-16:23

John 18:25-19:22

Psalm 119:113-128

Proverbs 16:10-11

All Access Pass — Day 151

Today's passages:

2 Samuel 17:1-29

John 19:23-42

Psalm 119:129-152

Proverbs 16:12-13

What verse spoke to you in this reading?

Do the New Testament and Old Testament passages have any similarities?

What other verses come to mind as you read these passages?

What questions do you still have? What do you want to know more about? What lesson or theme are you picking up on?

How can you apply these scriptures to your life? -

Today's prayers:

All Access Pass — Day 152

Today's passages:

2 Samuel 18:1-19:10

John 20:1-31

Psalm 119:153-176

Proverbs 16:14-15

What verse spoke to you in this reading?

Do the New Testament and Old Testament passages have any similarities?

What other verses come to mind as you read these passages?

What questions do you still have? What do you want to know more about? What lesson or theme are you picking up on?

How can you apply these scriptures to your life? -

Today's prayers:

All Access Pass — Day 153

Today's passages:

2 Samuel 19:11-20:13

John 21:1-25

Psalm 120:1-7

Proverbs 16:16-17

Notes

What verse spoke to you in this reading?

Do the New Testament and Old Testament passages have any similarities?

What other verses come to mind as you read these passages?

What questions do you still have? What do you want to know more about? What lesson or theme are you picking up on?

How can you apply these scriptures to your life? -

Today's prayers:

All Access Pass — Day 154

Today's passages:

2 Samuel 20:14-21:22

Acts 1:1-26

Psalm 121:1-8

Proverbs 16:18

What verse spoke to you in this reading?

Do the New Testament and Old Testament passages have any similarities?

What other verses come to mind as you read these passages?

What questions do you still have? What do you want to know more about? What lesson or theme are you picking up on?

How can you apply these scriptures to your life? -

Today's prayers:

All Access Pass — Day 155

Today's passages:

2 Samuel 22:1-23:23

Acts 2:1-47

Psalm 122:1-9

Proverbs 16:19-20

What verse spoke to you in this reading?

Do the New Testament and Old Testament passages have any similarities?

What other verses come to mind as you read these passages?

What questions do you still have? What do you want to know more about? What lesson or theme are you picking up on?

How can you apply these scriptures to your life? -

Today's prayers:

All Access Pass — Day 156

Today's passages:

2 Samuel 22:1-23:23

Acts 2:1-47

Psalm 122:1-9

Proverbs 16:19-20

What verse spoke to you in this reading?

Do the New Testament and Old Testament passages have any similarities?

What other verses come to mind as you read these passages?

What questions do you still have? What do you want to know more about? What lesson or theme are you picking up on?

How can you apply these scriptures to your life? -

Today's prayers:

All Access Pass — Day 157

Today's passages:

1 Kings 1:1-53

Acts 4:1-37

Psalm 124:1-8

Proverbs 16:24

Notes

What verse spoke to you in this reading?

Do the New Testament and Old Testament passages have any similarities?

What other verses come to mind as you read these passages?

What questions do you still have? What do you want to know more about? What lesson or theme are you picking up on?

How can you apply these scriptures to your life? -

Today's prayers:

All Access Pass — Day 158

Today's passages:

1 Kings 2:1-3:2

Acts 5:1-42

Psalm 125:1-5

Proverbs 16:25

Notes

What verse spoke to you in this reading?

Do the New Testament and Old Testament passages have any similarities?

What other verses come to mind as you read these passages?

What questions do you still have? What do you want to know more about? What lesson or theme are you picking up on?

How can you apply these scriptures to your life? -

Today's prayers:

All Access Pass — Day 159

Today's passages:

1 Kings 3:3-4:34

Acts 6:1-15

Psalm 126:1-6

Proverbs 16:26-27

Notes

What verse spoke to you in this reading?

Do the New Testament and Old Testament passages have any similarities?

What other verses come to mind as you read these passages?

What questions do you still have? What do you want to know more about? What lesson or theme are you picking up on?

How can you apply these scriptures to your life? -

Today's prayers:

All Access Pass — Day 160

What verse spoke to you in this reading?

Do the New Testament and Old Testament passages have any similarities?

What other verses come to mind as you read these passages?

What questions do you still have? What do you want to know more about? What lesson or theme are you picking up on?

How can you apply these scriptures to your life? -

Today's prayers:

Today's passages:

1 Kings 5:1-6:38

Acts 7:1-29

Psalm 127:1-5

Proverbs 16:28-30

Notes

All Access Pass — Day 161

Today's passages:

1 Kings 7:1-50

Acts 7:30-50

Psalm 128:1-6

Proverbs 16:31-33

Notes

What verse spoke to you in this reading?

Do the New Testament and Old Testament passages have any similarities?

What other verses come to mind as you read these passages?

What questions do you still have? What do you want to know more about? What lesson or theme are you picking up on?

How can you apply these scriptures to your life? -

Today's prayers:

All Access Pass — Day 162

What verse spoke to you in this reading?
___
___
___

Do the New Testament and Old Testament passages have any similarities?
___
___
___

What other verses come to mind as you read these passages?
___
___
___
___

What questions do you still have? What do you want to know more about? What lesson or theme are you picking up on?
___
___
___
___
___
___

How can you apply these scriptures to your life? -
___
___
___
___
___

Today's prayers:
___
___
___
___

Today's passages:

1 Kings 8:1-66

Acts 7:51-8:13

Psalm 129:1-8

Proverbs 17:1

Notes

All Access Pass — Day 163

Today's passages:

1 Kings 9:1-10:29

Acts 8:14-40

Psalm 130:1-8

Proverbs 17:2-3

Notes

What verse spoke to you in this reading?

Do the New Testament and Old Testament passages have any similarities?

What other verses come to mind as you read these passages?

What questions do you still have? What do you want to know more about? What lesson or theme are you picking up on?

How can you apply these scriptures to your life? -

Today's prayers:

All Access Pass — Day 164

Today's passages:

1 Kings 11:1-12:19

Acts 9:1-25

Psalm 131:1-3

Proverbs 17:4-5

Notes

What verse spoke to you in this reading?

Do the New Testament and Old Testament passages have any similarities?

What other verses come to mind as you read these passages?

What questions do you still have? What do you want to know more about? What lesson or theme are you picking up on?

How can you apply these scriptures to your life? -

Today's prayers:

All Access Pass — Day 165

Today's passages:

1 Kings 12:20-13:34

Acts 9:26-43

Psalm 132:1-18

Proverbs 17:6

Notes

What verse spoke to you in this reading?

Do the New Testament and Old Testament passages have any similarities?

What other verses come to mind as you read these passages?

What questions do you still have? What do you want to know more about? What lesson or theme are you picking up on?

How can you apply these scriptures to your life? -

Today's prayers:

All Access Pass — Day 166

What verse spoke to you in this reading?
_____
_____
_____

Do the New Testament and Old Testament passages have any similarities?
_____
_____
_____

What other verses come to mind as you read these passages?
_____
_____
_____

What questions do you still have? What do you want to know more about? What lesson or theme are you picking up on?
_____
_____
_____
_____
_____
_____

How can you apply these scriptures to your life? -
_____
_____
_____
_____

Today's prayers:
_____
_____
_____

Today's passages:

1 Kings 14:1-15:24

Acts 10:1-23

Psalm 133:1-3

Proverbs 17:7-8

Notes

All Access Pass — Day 167

Today's passages:

1 Kings 15:25-17:24

Acts 10:24-48

Psalm 134:1-3

Proverbs 17:9-11

Notes

What verse spoke to you in this reading?

Do the New Testament and Old Testament passages have any similarities?

What other verses come to mind as you read these passages?

What questions do you still have? What do you want to know more about? What lesson or theme are you picking up on?

How can you apply these scriptures to your life? -

Today's prayers:

All Access Pass — Day 168

Today's passages:

1 Kings 18:1-46

Acts 11:1-30

Psalm 135:1-21

Proverbs 17:12-13

Notes

What verse spoke to you in this reading?

Do the New Testament and Old Testament passages have any similarities?

What other verses come to mind as you read these passages?

What questions do you still have? What do you want to know more about? What lesson or theme are you picking up on?

How can you apply these scriptures to your life? -

Today's prayers:

All Access Pass — Day 169

Today's passages:

1 Kings 19:1-21

Acts 12:1-23

Psalm 136:1-26

Proverbs 17:14-15

Notes

What verse spoke to you in this reading?

Do the New Testament and Old Testament passages have any similarities?

What other verses come to mind as you read these passages?

What questions do you still have? What do you want to know more about? What lesson or theme are you picking up on?

How can you apply these scriptures to your life? -

Today's prayers:

All Access Pass — Day 170

Today's passages:

1 Kings 20:1-21:29

Acts 12:24-13:15

Psalm 137:1-9

Proverbs 17:16

Notes

What verse spoke to you in this reading?

Do the New Testament and Old Testament passages have any similarities?

What other verses come to mind as you read these passages?

What questions do you still have? What do you want to know more about? What lesson or theme are you picking up on?

How can you apply these scriptures to your life? -

Today's prayers:

All Access Pass — Day 171

Today's passages:

1 Kings 22:1-53

Acts 13:16-41

Psalm 138:1-8

Proverbs 17:17-18

Notes

What verse spoke to you in this reading?

Do the New Testament and Old Testament passages have any similarities?

What other verses come to mind as you read these passages?

What questions do you still have? What do you want to know more about? What lesson or theme are you picking up on?

How can you apply these scriptures to your life? -

Today's prayers:

All Access Pass — Day 172

What verse spoke to you in this reading?

Do the New Testament and Old Testament passages have any similarities?

What other verses come to mind as you read these passages?

What questions do you still have? What do you want to know more about? What lesson or theme are you picking up on?

How can you apply these scriptures to your life? -

Today's prayers:

Today's passages:

2 Kings 1:1-2:25

Acts 13:42-14:7

Psalm 139:1-24

Proverbs 17:19-21

Notes

All Access Pass — Day 173

Today's passages:

2 Kings 3:1-4:17

Acts 14:8-28

Psalm 140:1-13

Proverbs 17:22

Notes

What verse spoke to you in this reading?

Do the New Testament and Old Testament passages have any similarities?

What other verses come to mind as you read these passages?

What questions do you still have? What do you want to know more about? What lesson or theme are you picking up on?

How can you apply these scriptures to your life? -

Today's prayers:

All Access Pass — Day 174

Today's passages:

2 Kings 4:18-5:27

Acts 15:1-35

Psalm 141:1-10

Proverbs 17:23

Notes

What verse spoke to you in this reading?

Do the New Testament and Old Testament passages have any similarities?

What other verses come to mind as you read these passages?

What questions do you still have? What do you want to know more about? What lesson or theme are you picking up on?

How can you apply these scriptures to your life? -

Today's prayers:

All Access Pass — Day 175

Today's passages:

2 Kings 4:18-5:27

Acts 15:1-35

Psalm 141:1-10

Proverbs 17:23

What verse spoke to you in this reading?

Do the New Testament and Old Testament passages have any similarities?

What other verses come to mind as you read these passages?

What questions do you still have? What do you want to know more about? What lesson or theme are you picking up on?

How can you apply these scriptures to your life? -

Today's prayers:

All Access Pass — Day 176

Today's passages:

2 Kings 8:1-9:13

Acts 16:16-40

Psalm 143:1-12

Proverbs 17:26

Notes

What verse spoke to you in this reading?

Do the New Testament and Old Testament passages have any similarities?

What other verses come to mind as you read these passages?

What questions do you still have? What do you want to know more about? What lesson or theme are you picking up on?

How can you apply these scriptures to your life? -

Today's prayers:

All Access Pass — Day 177

Today's passages:

2 Kings 9:14-10:31

Acts 17:1-34

Psalm 144:1-15

Proverbs 17:27-28

Notes

What verse spoke to you in this reading?

Do the New Testament and Old Testament passages have any similarities?

What other verses come to mind as you read these passages?

What questions do you still have? What do you want to know more about? What lesson or theme are you picking up on?

How can you apply these scriptures to your life? -

Today's prayers:

All Access Pass — Day 178

Today's passages:

2 Kings 10:32-12:21

Acts 18:1-22

Psalm 145:1-21

Proverbs 18:1

Notes

What verse spoke to you in this reading?

Do the New Testament and Old Testament passages have any similarities?

What other verses come to mind as you read these passages?

What questions do you still have? What do you want to know more about? What lesson or theme are you picking up on?

How can you apply these scriptures to your life? -

Today's prayers:

All Access Pass — Day 179

Today's passages:

2 Kings 13:1-14:29

Acts 18:23-19:12

Psalm 146:1-10

Proverbs 18:2-3

Notes

What verse spoke to you in this reading?

Do the New Testament and Old Testament passages have any similarities?

What other verses come to mind as you read these passages?

What questions do you still have? What do you want to know more about? What lesson or theme are you picking up on?

How can you apply these scriptures to your life? -

Today's prayers:

All Access Pass — Day 180

What verse spoke to you in this reading?

Do the New Testament and Old Testament passages have any similarities?

What other verses come to mind as you read these passages?

What questions do you still have? What do you want to know more about? What lesson or theme are you picking up on?

How can you apply these scriptures to your life? -

Today's prayers:

Today's passages:

2 Kings 15:1-16:20

Acts 19:13-41

Psalm 147:1-20

Proverbs 18:4-5

Notes

All Access Pass — Day 181

Today's passages:

2 Kings 17:1-18:12

Acts 20:1-38

Psalm 148:1-14

Proverbs 18:6-7

Notes

What verse spoke to you in this reading?

Do the New Testament and Old Testament passages have any similarities?

What other verses come to mind as you read these passages?

What questions do you still have? What do you want to know more about? What lesson or theme are you picking up on?

How can you apply these scriptures to your life? -

Today's prayers:

All Access Pass — Day 182

What verse spoke to you in this reading?

Do the New Testament and Old Testament passages have any similarities?

What other verses come to mind as you read these passages?

What questions do you still have? What do you want to know more about? What lesson or theme are you picking up on?

How can you apply these scriptures to your life? -

Today's prayers:

Today's passages:

2 Kings 18:13-19:37

Acts 21:1-17

Psalm 149:1-9

Proverbs 18:8

Notes

All Access Pass — Day 183

Today's passages:

2 Kings 20:1-22:2

Acts 21:18-36

Psalm 150:1-6

Proverbs 18:9-10

Notes

What verse spoke to you in this reading?

Do the New Testament and Old Testament passages have any similarities?

What other verses come to mind as you read these passages?

What questions do you still have? What do you want to know more about? What lesson or theme are you picking up on?

How can you apply these scriptures to your life? -

Today's prayers:

All Access Pass — Day 184

Today's passages:

2 Kings 22:3-23:30

Acts 21:37-22:16

Psalm 1:1-6

Proverbs 18:11-12

Notes

What verse spoke to you in this reading?

Do the New Testament and Old Testament passages have any similarities?

What other verses come to mind as you read these passages?

What questions do you still have? What do you want to know more about? What lesson or theme are you picking up on?

How can you apply these scriptures to your life? -

Today's prayers:

All Access Pass — Day 185

Today's passages:

2 Kings 23:31-25:30

Acts 22:17-23:10

Psalm 2:1-12

Proverbs 18:13

Notes

What verse spoke to you in this reading?

Do the New Testament and Old Testament passages have any similarities?

What other verses come to mind as you read these passages?

What questions do you still have? What do you want to know more about? What lesson or theme are you picking up on?

How can you apply these scriptures to your life? -

Today's prayers:

All Access Pass — Day 186

What verse spoke to you in this reading?

Do the New Testament and Old Testament passages have any similarities?

What other verses come to mind as you read these passages?

What questions do you still have? What do you want to know more about? What lesson or theme are you picking up on?

How can you apply these scriptures to your life? -

Today's prayers:

Today's passages:

1 Chronicles 1:1-2:17

Acts 23:11-35

Psalm 3:1-8

Proverbs 18:14-15

Notes

All Access Pass — Day 187

Today's passages:

1 Chronicles 2:18-4:4

Acts 24:1-27

Psalm 4:1-8

Proverbs 18:16-18

What verse spoke to you in this reading?

Do the New Testament and Old Testament passages have any similarities?

What other verses come to mind as you read these passages?

What questions do you still have? What do you want to know more about? What lesson or theme are you picking up on?

How can you apply these scriptures to your life? -

Today's prayers:

All Access Pass — Day 188

Today's passages:

1 Chronicles 4:5-5:17

Acts 25:1-27

Psalm 5:1-12

Proverbs 18:19

What verse spoke to you in this reading?

Do the New Testament and Old Testament passages have any similarities?

What other verses come to mind as you read these passages?

What questions do you still have? What do you want to know more about? What lesson or theme are you picking up on?

How can you apply these scriptures to your life? -

Today's prayers:

All Access Pass — Day 189

Today's passages:

1 Chronicles 5:18-6:81

Acts 26:1-32

Psalm 6:1-10

Proverbs 18:20-21

Notes

What verse spoke to you in this reading?

Do the New Testament and Old Testament passages have any similarities?

What other verses come to mind as you read these passages?

What questions do you still have? What do you want to know more about? What lesson or theme are you picking up on?

How can you apply these scriptures to your life? -

Today's prayers:

All Access Pass — Day 190

Today's passages:

1 Chronicles 7:1-8:40

Acts 27:1-20

Psalm 7:1-17

Proverbs 18:22

Notes

What verse spoke to you in this reading?

Do the New Testament and Old Testament passages have any similarities?

What other verses come to mind as you read these passages?

What questions do you still have? What do you want to know more about? What lesson or theme are you picking up on?

How can you apply these scriptures to your life? -

Today's prayers:

All Access Pass — Day 191

Today's passages:

1 Chronicles 9:1-10:14

Acts 27:21-44

Psalm 8:1-9

Proverbs 18:23-24

What verse spoke to you in this reading?

Do the New Testament and Old Testament passages have any similarities?

What other verses come to mind as you read these passages?

What questions do you still have? What do you want to know more about? What lesson or theme are you picking up on?

How can you apply these scriptures to your life? -

Today's prayers:

All Access Pass — Day 192

Today's passages:

1 Chronicles 11:1-12:18

Acts 28:1-31

Psalm 9:1-12

Proverbs 19:1-3

Notes

What verse spoke to you in this reading?

Do the New Testament and Old Testament passages have any similarities?

What other verses come to mind as you read these passages?

What questions do you still have? What do you want to know more about? What lesson or theme are you picking up on?

How can you apply these scriptures to your life? -

Today's prayers:

All Access Pass — Day 193

Today's passages:

1 Chronicles 12:19-14:17

Romans 1:1-17

Psalm 9:13-20

Proverbs 19:4-5

What verse spoke to you in this reading?

Do the New Testament and Old Testament passages have any similarities?

What other verses come to mind as you read these passages?

What questions do you still have? What do you want to know more about? What lesson or theme are you picking up on?

How can you apply these scriptures to your life? -

Today's prayers:

All Access Pass — Day 194

Today's passages:

1 Chronicles 15:1-16:36

Romans 1:18-32

Psalm 10:1-15

Proverbs 19:6-7

Notes

What verse spoke to you in this reading?

Do the New Testament and Old Testament passages have any similarities?

What other verses come to mind as you read these passages?

What questions do you still have? What do you want to know more about? What lesson or theme are you picking up on?

How can you apply these scriptures to your life? -

Today's prayers:

All Access Pass — Day 195

Today's passages:

1 Chronicles 16:37-18:17

Romans 2:1-24

Psalm 10:16-18

Proverbs 19:8-9

Notes

What verse spoke to you in this reading?

Do the New Testament and Old Testament passages have any similarities?

What other verses come to mind as you read these passages?

What questions do you still have? What do you want to know more about? What lesson or theme are you picking up on?

How can you apply these scriptures to your life? -

Today's prayers:

All Access Pass — Day 196

What verse spoke to you in this reading?

Do the New Testament and Old Testament passages have any similarities?

What other verses come to mind as you read these passages?

What questions do you still have? What do you want to know more about? What lesson or theme are you picking up on?

How can you apply these scriptures to your life? -

Today's prayers:

Today's passages:

1 Chronicles 19:1-21:30

Romans 2:25-3:8

Psalm 11:1-7

Proverbs 19:10-12

Notes

All Access Pass — Day 197

Today's passages:

1 Chronicles 22:1-23:32

Romans 3:9-31

Psalm 12:1-8

Proverbs 19:13-14

Notes

What verse spoke to you in this reading?

Do the New Testament and Old Testament passages have any similarities?

What other verses come to mind as you read these passages?

What questions do you still have? What do you want to know more about? What lesson or theme are you picking up on?

How can you apply these scriptures to your life? -

Today's prayers:

All Access Pass — Day 198

Today's passages:

1 Chronicles 24:1-26:11

Romans 4:1-12

Psalm 13:1-6

Proverbs 19:15-16

Notes

What verse spoke to you in this reading?

Do the New Testament and Old Testament passages have any similarities?

What other verses come to mind as you read these passages?

What questions do you still have? What do you want to know more about? What lesson or theme are you picking up on?

How can you apply these scriptures to your life? -

Today's prayers:

All Access Pass — Day 199

Today's passages:

1 Chronicles 26:12-27:34

Romans 4:13-5:5

Psalm 14:1-7

Proverbs 19:17

Notes

What verse spoke to you in this reading?

Do the New Testament and Old Testament passages have any similarities?

What other verses come to mind as you read these passages?

What questions do you still have? What do you want to know more about? What lesson or theme are you picking up on?

How can you apply these scriptures to your life? -

Today's prayers:

All Access Pass — Day 200

What verse spoke to you in this reading?

Do the New Testament and Old Testament passages have any similarities?

What other verses come to mind as you read these passages?

What questions do you still have? What do you want to know more about? What lesson or theme are you picking up on?

How can you apply these scriptures to your life? -

Today's prayers:

Today's passages:

1 Chronicles 28:1-29:30

Romans 5:6-21

Psalm 15:1-5

Proverbs 19:18-19

Notes

All Access Pass — Day 201

Today's passages:

2 Chronicles 1:1-3:17

Romans 6:1-23

Psalm 16:1-11

Proverbs 19:20-21

Notes

What verse spoke to you in this reading?

Do the New Testament and Old Testament passages have any similarities?

What other verses come to mind as you read these passages?

What questions do you still have? What do you want to know more about? What lesson or theme are you picking up on?

How can you apply these scriptures to your life? -

Today's prayers:

All Access Pass — Day 202

Today's passages:

2 Chronicles 4:1-6:11

Romans 7:1-13

Psalm 17:1-15

Proverbs 19:22-23

What verse spoke to you in this reading?

Do the New Testament and Old Testament passages have any similarities?

What other verses come to mind as you read these passages?

What questions do you still have? What do you want to know more about? What lesson or theme are you picking up on?

How can you apply these scriptures to your life? -

Today's prayers:

All Access Pass — Day 203

Today's passages:

2 Chronicles 6:12-8:10

Romans 7:14-8:8

Psalm 18:1-15

Proverbs 19:24-25

Notes

What verse spoke to you in this reading?

Do the New Testament and Old Testament passages have any similarities?

What other verses come to mind as you read these passages?

What questions do you still have? What do you want to know more about? What lesson or theme are you picking up on?

How can you apply these scriptures to your life? -

Today's prayers:

All Access Pass — Day 204

What verse spoke to you in this reading?

Do the New Testament and Old Testament passages have any similarities?

What other verses come to mind as you read these passages?

What questions do you still have? What do you want to know more about? What lesson or theme are you picking up on?

How can you apply these scriptures to your life? -

Today's prayers:

Today's passages:

2 Chronicles 8:11-10:19

Romans 8:9-25

Psalm 18:16-36

Proverbs 19:26

Notes

All Access Pass — Day 205

Today's passages:

2 Chronicles 11:1-13:22

Romans 8:26-39

Psalm 18:37-50

Proverbs 19:27-29

Notes

What verse spoke to you in this reading?

Do the New Testament and Old Testament passages have any similarities?

What other verses come to mind as you read these passages?

What questions do you still have? What do you want to know more about? What lesson or theme are you picking up on?

How can you apply these scriptures to your life? -

Today's prayers:

All Access Pass — Day 206

Today's passages:

2 Chronicles 14:1-16:14

Romans 9:1-24

Psalm 19:1-14

Proverbs 20:1

Notes

What verse spoke to you in this reading?

Do the New Testament and Old Testament passages have any similarities?

What other verses come to mind as you read these passages?

What questions do you still have? What do you want to know more about? What lesson or theme are you picking up on?

How can you apply these scriptures to your life? -

Today's prayers:

All Access Pass — Day 207

Today's passages:

2 Chronicles 17:1-18:34

Romans 9:25-10:13

Psalm 20:1-9

Proverbs 20:2-3

Notes

What verse spoke to you in this reading?

Do the New Testament and Old Testament passages have any similarities?

What other verses come to mind as you read these passages?

What questions do you still have? What do you want to know more about? What lesson or theme are you picking up on?

How can you apply these scriptures to your life? -

Today's prayers:

All Access Pass — Day 208

What verse spoke to you in this reading?

Do the New Testament and Old Testament passages have any similarities?

What other verses come to mind as you read these passages?

What questions do you still have? What do you want to know more about? What lesson or theme are you picking up on?

How can you apply these scriptures to your life? -

Today's prayers:

Today's passages:

2 Chronicles 19:1-20:37

Romans 10:14-11:12

Psalm 21:1-13

Proverbs 20:4-6

Notes

All Access Pass — Day 209

Today's passages:

2 Chronicles 21:1-23:21

Romans 11:13-36

Psalm 22:1-18

Proverbs 20:7

Notes

What verse spoke to you in this reading?

Do the New Testament and Old Testament passages have any similarities?

What other verses come to mind as you read these passages?

What questions do you still have? What do you want to know more about? What lesson or theme are you picking up on?

How can you apply these scriptures to your life? -

Today's prayers:

All Access Pass — Day 210

Today's passages:

2 Chronicles 24:1-25:28

Romans 12:1-21

Psalm 22:19-31

Proverbs 20:8-10

What verse spoke to you in this reading?

Do the New Testament and Old Testament passages have any similarities?

What other verses come to mind as you read these passages?

What questions do you still have? What do you want to know more about? What lesson or theme are you picking up on?

How can you apply these scriptures to your life? -

Today's prayers:

All Access Pass — Day 211

Today's passages:

2 Chronicles 26:1-28:27

Romans 13:1-14

Psalm 23:1-6

Proverbs 20:11

Notes

What verse spoke to you in this reading?

Do the New Testament and Old Testament passages have any similarities?

What other verses come to mind as you read these passages?

What questions do you still have? What do you want to know more about? What lesson or theme are you picking up on?

How can you apply these scriptures to your life? -

Today's prayers:

All Access Pass — Day 212

What verse spoke to you in this reading?

Do the New Testament and Old Testament passages have any similarities?

What other verses come to mind as you read these passages?

What questions do you still have? What do you want to know more about? What lesson or theme are you picking up on?

How can you apply these scriptures to your life? -

Today's prayers:

Today's passages:

2 Chronicles 29:1-36

Romans 14:1-23

Psalm 24:1-10

Proverbs 20:12

Notes

All Access Pass — Day 213

Today's passages:

2 Chronicles 30:1-31:21

Romans 15:1-22

Psalm 25:1-15

Proverbs 20:13-15

Notes

What verse spoke to you in this reading?

Do the New Testament and Old Testament passages have any similarities?

What other verses come to mind as you read these passages?

What questions do you still have? What do you want to know more about? What lesson or theme are you picking up on?

How can you apply these scriptures to your life? -

Today's prayers:

All Access Pass — Day 214

What verse spoke to you in this reading?

Do the New Testament and Old Testament passages have any similarities?

What other verses come to mind as you read these passages?

What questions do you still have? What do you want to know more about? What lesson or theme are you picking up on?

How can you apply these scriptures to your life? -

Today's prayers:

Today's passages:

2 Chronicles 32:1-33:13

Romans 15:23-16:9

Psalm 25:16-22

Proverbs 20:16-18

Notes

All Access Pass — Day 215

Today's passages:

2 Chronicles 33:14-34:33

Romans 16:10-27

Psalm 26:1-12

Proverbs 20:19

What verse spoke to you in this reading?
_____
_____
_____

Do the New Testament and Old Testament passages have any similarities?
_____
_____
_____

What other verses come to mind as you read these passages?
_____
_____
_____

What questions do you still have? What do you want to know more about? What lesson or theme are you picking up on?
_____
_____
_____
_____
_____
_____

How can you apply these scriptures to your life? -
_____
_____
_____
_____

Today's prayers:
_____
_____
_____

All Access Pass — Day 216

Today's passages:

2 Chronicles 35:1-36:23

1 Corinthians 1:1-17

Psalm 27:1-6

Proverbs 20:20-21

Notes

What verse spoke to you in this reading?

Do the New Testament and Old Testament passages have any similarities?

What other verses come to mind as you read these passages?

What questions do you still have? What do you want to know more about? What lesson or theme are you picking up on?

How can you apply these scriptures to your life? -

Today's prayers:

All Access Pass — Day 217

Today's passages:

Ezra 1:1-2:70

1 Corinthians 1:18-2:5

Psalm 27:7-14

Proverbs 20:22-23

Notes

What verse spoke to you in this reading?

Do the New Testament and Old Testament passages have any similarities?

What other verses come to mind as you read these passages?

What questions do you still have? What do you want to know more about? What lesson or theme are you picking up on?

How can you apply these scriptures to your life? -

Today's prayers:

All Access Pass — Day 218

Today's passages:

Ezra 3:1-4:23

1 Corinthians 2:6-3:4

Psalm 28:1-9

Proverbs 20:24-25

Notes

What verse spoke to you in this reading?

Do the New Testament and Old Testament passages have any similarities?

What other verses come to mind as you read these passages?

What questions do you still have? What do you want to know more about? What lesson or theme are you picking up on?

How can you apply these scriptures to your life? -

Today's prayers:

All Access Pass — Day 219

Today's passages:

Ezra 4:24-6:22

1 Corinthians 3:5-23

Psalm 29:1-11

Proverbs 20:26-27

What verse spoke to you in this reading?

Do the New Testament and Old Testament passages have any similarities?

What other verses come to mind as you read these passages?

What questions do you still have? What do you want to know more about? What lesson or theme are you picking up on?

How can you apply these scriptures to your life? -

Today's prayers:

All Access Pass — Day 220

Today's passages:

Ezra 7:1-8:20

1 Corinthians 4:1-21

Psalm 30:1-12

Proverbs 20:28-30

Notes

What verse spoke to you in this reading?

Do the New Testament and Old Testament passages have any similarities?

What other verses come to mind as you read these passages?

What questions do you still have? What do you want to know more about? What lesson or theme are you picking up on?

How can you apply these scriptures to your life? -

Today's prayers:

All Access Pass — Day 221

Today's passages:

Ezra 8:21-9:15

1 Corinthians 5:1-13

Psalm 31:1-8

Proverbs 21:1-2

Notes

What verse spoke to you in this reading?

Do the New Testament and Old Testament passages have any similarities?

What other verses come to mind as you read these passages?

What questions do you still have? What do you want to know more about? What lesson or theme are you picking up on?

How can you apply these scriptures to your life? -

Today's prayers:

All Access Pass — Day 222

What verse spoke to you in this reading?

Do the New Testament and Old Testament passages have any similarities?

What other verses come to mind as you read these passages?

What questions do you still have? What do you want to know more about? What lesson or theme are you picking up on?

How can you apply these scriptures to your life? -

Today's prayers:

Today's passages:

Ezra 10:1-44

1 Corinthians 6:1-20

Psalm 31:9-18

Proverbs 21:3

Notes

All Access Pass — Day 223

Today's passages:

Nehemiah 1:1-3:14

1 Corinthians 7:1-24

Psalm 31:19-24

Proverbs 21:4

What verse spoke to you in this reading?

Do the New Testament and Old Testament passages have any similarities?

What other verses come to mind as you read these passages?

What questions do you still have? What do you want to know more about? What lesson or theme are you picking up on?

How can you apply these scriptures to your life? -

Today's prayers:

All Access Pass — Day 224

Today's passages:

Nehemiah 3:15-5:13

1 Corinthians 7:25-40

Psalm 32:1-11

Proverbs 21:5-7

Notes

What verse spoke to you in this reading?

Do the New Testament and Old Testament passages have any similarities?

What other verses come to mind as you read these passages?

What questions do you still have? What do you want to know more about? What lesson or theme are you picking up on?

How can you apply these scriptures to your life? -

Today's prayers:

All Access Pass — Day 225

Today's passages:

Nehemiah 5:14-7:73

1 Corinthians 8:1-13

Psalm 33:1-11

Proverbs 21:8-10

Notes

What verse spoke to you in this reading?

Do the New Testament and Old Testament passages have any similarities?

What other verses come to mind as you read these passages?

What questions do you still have? What do you want to know more about? What lesson or theme are you picking up on?

How can you apply these scriptures to your life? -

Today's prayers:

All Access Pass — Day 226

Today's passages:

Nehemiah 7:73-9:21

1 Corinthians 9:1-18

Psalm 33:12-22

Proverbs 21:11-12

Notes

What verse spoke to you in this reading?

Do the New Testament and Old Testament passages have any similarities?

What other verses come to mind as you read these passages?

What questions do you still have? What do you want to know more about? What lesson or theme are you picking up on?

How can you apply these scriptures to your life? -

Today's prayers:

All Access Pass — Day 227

Today's passages:

Nehemiah 9:22-10:39

1 Corinthians 9:19-10:13

Psalm 34:1-10

Proverbs 21:13

Notes

What verse spoke to you in this reading?

Do the New Testament and Old Testament passages have any similarities?

What other verses come to mind as you read these passages?

What questions do you still have? What do you want to know more about? What lesson or theme are you picking up on?

How can you apply these scriptures to your life? -

Today's prayers:

All Access Pass — Day 228

What verse spoke to you in this reading?

Do the New Testament and Old Testament passages have any similarities?

What other verses come to mind as you read these passages?

What questions do you still have? What do you want to know more about? What lesson or theme are you picking up on?

How can you apply these scriptures to your life? -

Today's prayers:

Today's passages:

Nehemiah 11:1-12:26

1 Corinthians 10:14-33

Psalm 34:11-22

Proverbs 21:14-16

Notes

All Access Pass — Day 229

Today's passages:

Nehemiah 12:27-13:31

1 Corinthians 11:1-16

Psalm 35:1-16

Proverbs 21:17-18

Notes

What verse spoke to you in this reading?

Do the New Testament and Old Testament passages have any similarities?

What other verses come to mind as you read these passages?

What questions do you still have? What do you want to know more about? What lesson or theme are you picking up on?

How can you apply these scriptures to your life? -

Today's prayers:

All Access Pass — Day 230

Today's passages:

Esther 1:1-3:15

1 Corinthians 11:17-34

Psalm 35:17-28

Proverbs 21:19-20

Notes

What verse spoke to you in this reading?

Do the New Testament and Old Testament passages have any similarities?

What other verses come to mind as you read these passages?

What questions do you still have? What do you want to know more about? What lesson or theme are you picking up on?

How can you apply these scriptures to your life? -

Today's prayers:

All Access Pass — Day 231

Today's passages:

Esther 4:1-7:10

1 Corinthians 12:1-26

Psalm 36:1-12

Proverbs 21:21-22

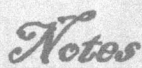

What verse spoke to you in this reading?

Do the New Testament and Old Testament passages have any similarities?

What other verses come to mind as you read these passages?

What questions do you still have? What do you want to know more about? What lesson or theme are you picking up on?

How can you apply these scriptures to your life? -

Today's prayers:

All Access Pass — Day 232

Today's passages:

Esther 8:1-10:3

1 Corinthians 12:27-13:13

Psalm 37:1-11

Proverbs 21:23-24

Notes

What verse spoke to you in this reading?

Do the New Testament and Old Testament passages have any similarities?

What other verses come to mind as you read these passages?

What questions do you still have? What do you want to know more about? What lesson or theme are you picking up on?

How can you apply these scriptures to your life? -

Today's prayers:

All Access Pass — Day 233

Today's passages:

Job 1:1-3:26

1 Corinthians 14:1-17

Psalm 37:12-29

Proverbs 21:25-26

Notes

What verse spoke to you in this reading?

Do the New Testament and Old Testament passages have any similarities?

What other verses come to mind as you read these passages?

What questions do you still have? What do you want to know more about? What lesson or theme are you picking up on?

How can you apply these scriptures to your life? -

Today's prayers:

All Access Pass — Day 234

Today's passages:

Job 4:1-7:21

1 Corinthians 14:18-40

Psalm 37:30-40

Proverbs 21:27

Notes

What verse spoke to you in this reading?

Do the New Testament and Old Testament passages have any similarities?

What other verses come to mind as you read these passages?

What questions do you still have? What do you want to know more about? What lesson or theme are you picking up on?

How can you apply these scriptures to your life? -

Today's prayers:

All Access Pass — Day 235

Today's passages:

Job 8:1-11:20

1 Corinthians 15:1-28

Psalm 38:1-22

Proverbs 21:28-29

What verse spoke to you in this reading?

Do the New Testament and Old Testament passages have any similarities?

What other verses come to mind as you read these passages?

What questions do you still have? What do you want to know more about? What lesson or theme are you picking up on?

How can you apply these scriptures to your life? -

Today's prayers:

All Access Pass — Day 236

Today's passages:

Job 12:1-15:35

1 Corinthians 15:29-58

Psalm 39:1-13

Proverbs 21:30-31

Notes

What verse spoke to you in this reading?

Do the New Testament and Old Testament passages have any similarities?

What other verses come to mind as you read these passages?

What questions do you still have? What do you want to know more about? What lesson or theme are you picking up on?

How can you apply these scriptures to your life? -

Today's prayers:

All Access Pass — Day 237

Today's passages:

Job 16:1-19:29

1 Corinthians 16:1-24

Psalm 40:1-10

Proverbs 22:1

Notes

What verse spoke to you in this reading?

Do the New Testament and Old Testament passages have any similarities?

What other verses come to mind as you read these passages?

What questions do you still have? What do you want to know more about? What lesson or theme are you picking up on?

How can you apply these scriptures to your life? -

Today's prayers:

All Access Pass — Day 238

What verse spoke to you in this reading?

Do the New Testament and Old Testament passages have any similarities?

What other verses come to mind as you read these passages?

What questions do you still have? What do you want to know more about? What lesson or theme are you picking up on?

How can you apply these scriptures to your life? -

Today's prayers:

Today's passages:

Job 20:1-22:30

2 Corinthians 1:1-11

Psalm 40:11-17

Proverbs 22:2-4

Notes

All Access Pass — Day 239

Today's passages:

Job 23:1-27:23

2 Corinthians 1:12-2:11

Psalm 41:1-13

Proverbs 22:5-6

Notes

What verse spoke to you in this reading?

Do the New Testament and Old Testament passages have any similarities?

What other verses come to mind as you read these passages?

What questions do you still have? What do you want to know more about? What lesson or theme are you picking up on?

How can you apply these scriptures to your life? -

Today's prayers:

 **Day 240**

What verse spoke to you in this reading?

Do the New Testament and Old Testament passages have any similarities?

What other verses come to mind as you read these passages?

What questions do you still have? What do you want to know more about? What lesson or theme are you picking up on?

How can you apply these scriptures to your life? -

Today's prayers:

Today's passages:

Job 28:1-30:31

2 Corinthians 2:12-17

Psalm 42:1-11

Proverbs 22:7

All Access Pass — Day 241

Today's passages:

Job 31:1-33:33

2 Corinthians 3:1-18

Psalm 43:1-5

Proverbs 22:8-9

Notes

What verse spoke to you in this reading?

Do the New Testament and Old Testament passages have any similarities?

What other verses come to mind as you read these passages?

What questions do you still have? What do you want to know more about? What lesson or theme are you picking up on?

How can you apply these scriptures to your life? -

Today's prayers:

All Access Pass — Day 242

Today's passages:

Job 34:1-36:33

2 Corinthians 4:1-12

Psalm 44:1-8

Proverbs 22:10-12

What verse spoke to you in this reading?

Do the New Testament and Old Testament passages have any similarities?

What other verses come to mind as you read these passages?

What questions do you still have? What do you want to know more about? What lesson or theme are you picking up on?

How can you apply these scriptures to your life? -

Today's prayers:

All Access Pass — Day 243

Today's passages:

Job 37:1-39:30

2 Corinthians 4:13-5:10

Psalm 44:9-26

Proverbs 22:13

Notes

What verse spoke to you in this reading?

Do the New Testament and Old Testament passages have any similarities?

What other verses come to mind as you read these passages?

What questions do you still have? What do you want to know more about? What lesson or theme are you picking up on?

How can you apply these scriptures to your life? -

Today's prayers:

All Access Pass — Day 244

Today's passages:

Job 40:1-42:17

2 Corinthians 5:11-21

Psalm 45:1-17

Proverbs 22:14

Notes

What verse spoke to you in this reading?

Do the New Testament and Old Testament passages have any similarities?

What other verses come to mind as you read these passages?

What questions do you still have? What do you want to know more about? What lesson or theme are you picking up on?

How can you apply these scriptures to your life? -

Today's prayers:

All Access Pass — Day 245

Today's passages:

Ecclesiastes 1:1-3:22

2 Corinthians 6:1-13

Psalm 46:1-11

Proverbs 22:15

Notes

What verse spoke to you in this reading?

Do the New Testament and Old Testament passages have any similarities?

What other verses come to mind as you read these passages?

What questions do you still have? What do you want to know more about? What lesson or theme are you picking up on?

How can you apply these scriptures to your life? -

Today's prayers:

All Access Pass — Day 246

Today's passages:

Ecclesiastes 4:1-6:12

2 Corinthians 6:14-7:7

Psalm 47:1-9

Proverbs 22:16

Notes

What verse spoke to you in this reading?

Do the New Testament and Old Testament passages have any similarities?

What other verses come to mind as you read these passages?

What questions do you still have? What do you want to know more about? What lesson or theme are you picking up on?

How can you apply these scriptures to your life? -

Today's prayers:

All Access Pass — Day 247

Today's passages:

Ecclesiastes 7:1-9:18

2 Corinthians 7:8-16

Psalm 48:1-14

Proverbs 22:17-19

Notes

What verse spoke to you in this reading?

Do the New Testament and Old Testament passages have any similarities?

What other verses come to mind as you read these passages?

What questions do you still have? What do you want to know more about? What lesson or theme are you picking up on?

How can you apply these scriptures to your life? -

Today's prayers:

All Access Pass — Day 248

Today's passages:

Ecclesiastes 10:1-12:14

2 Corinthians 8;1-15

Psalm 49:1-20

Proverbs 22:20-21

Notes

What verse spoke to you in this reading?

Do the New Testament and Old Testament passages have any similarities?

What other verses come to mind as you read these passages?

What questions do you still have? What do you want to know more about? What lesson or theme are you picking up on?

How can you apply these scriptures to your life? -

Today's prayers:

All Access Pass — Day 249

Today's passages:

Song of Solomon 1:1-4:16

2 Corinthians 8:16-24

Psalm 50:1-23

Proverbs 22;22-23

Notes

What verse spoke to you in this reading?

Do the New Testament and Old Testament passages have any similarities?

What other verses come to mind as you read these passages?

What questions do you still have? What do you want to know more about? What lesson or theme are you picking up on?

How can you apply these scriptures to your life? -

Today's prayers:

 **Day 250**

What verse spoke to you in this reading?

Do the New Testament and Old Testament passages have any similarities?

What other verses come to mind as you read these passages?

What questions do you still have? What do you want to know more about? What lesson or theme are you picking up on?

How can you apply these scriptures to your life? -

Today's prayers:

Today's passages:

Song of Solomon 5:1-8:14

2 Corinthians 9:1-15

Psalm 51:1-19

Proverbs 22:24-25

All Access Pass  Day 251

Today's passages:

Isaiah 1:1-2:22

2 Corinthians 10:1-18

Psalm 52:1-9

Proverbs 22:26-27

What verse spoke to you in this reading?

Do the New Testament and Old Testament passages have any similarities?

What other verses come to mind as you read these passages?

What questions do you still have? What do you want to know more about? What lesson or theme are you picking up on?

How can you apply these scriptures to your life? -

Today's prayers:

All Access Pass — Day 252

What verse spoke to you in this reading?

Do the New Testament and Old Testament passages have any similarities?

What other verses come to mind as you read these passages?

What questions do you still have? What do you want to know more about? What lesson or theme are you picking up on?

How can you apply these scriptures to your life? -

Today's prayers:

Today's passages:

Isaiah 3:1-5:30

2 Corinthians 11:1-15

Psalm 53:1-6

Proverbs 22:28-29

Notes

All Access Pass — Day 253

Today's passages:

Isaiah 6:1-7:25

2 Corinthians 11:16-33

Psalm 54:1-7

Proverbs 23:1-3

Notes

What verse spoke to you in this reading?

Do the New Testament and Old Testament passages have any similarities?

What other verses come to mind as you read these passages?

What questions do you still have? What do you want to know more about? What lesson or theme are you picking up on?

How can you apply these scriptures to your life? -

Today's prayers:

All Access Pass — Day 254

What verse spoke to you in this reading?

Do the New Testament and Old Testament passages have any similarities?

What other verses come to mind as you read these passages?

What questions do you still have? What do you want to know more about? What lesson or theme are you picking up on?

How can you apply these scriptures to your life? -

Today's prayers:

Today's passages:

Isaiah 8:1-9:21

2 Corinthians 12:1-10

Psalm 55:1-23

Proverbs 23:4-5

Notes

All Access Pass — Day 255

Today's passages:

Isaiah 10:1-11:16

2 Corinthians 12;11-21

Psalm 56:1-13

Proverbs 23:6-8

Notes

What verse spoke to you in this reading?

Do the New Testament and Old Testament passages have any similarities?

What other verses come to mind as you read these passages?

What questions do you still have? What do you want to know more about? What lesson or theme are you picking up on?

How can you apply these scriptures to your life? -

Today's prayers:

All Access Pass — Day 256

What verse spoke to you in this reading?

Do the New Testament and Old Testament passages have any similarities?

What other verses come to mind as you read these passages?

What questions do you still have? What do you want to know more about? What lesson or theme are you picking up on?

How can you apply these scriptures to your life? -

Today's prayers:

Today's passages:

Isaiah 12:1-14:32

2 Corinthians 13:1-14

Psalm 57:1-11

Proverbs 23:9-11

Notes

All Access Pass — Day 257

Today's passages:

Isaiah 15:1-18:7

Galatians 1:1-24

Psalm 58:1-11

Proverbs 23:12

Notes

What verse spoke to you in this reading?

Do the New Testament and Old Testament passages have any similarities?

What other verses come to mind as you read these passages?

What questions do you still have? What do you want to know more about? What lesson or theme are you picking up on?

How can you apply these scriptures to your life? -

Today's prayers:

All Access Pass — Day 258

What verse spoke to you in this reading?

Do the New Testament and Old Testament passages have any similarities?

What other verses come to mind as you read these passages?

What questions do you still have? What do you want to know more about? What lesson or theme are you picking up on?

How can you apply these scriptures to your life? -

Today's prayers:

Today's passages:

Isaiah 19:1-21:17

Galatians 2:1-16

Psalm 59:1-17

Proverbs 23:13-14

Notes

All Access Pass — Day 259

Today's passages:

Isaiah 22:1-24:23

Galatians 2:17-3:9

Psalm 60:1-12

Proverbs 23:15-16

Notes

What verse spoke to you in this reading?

Do the New Testament and Old Testament passages have any similarities?

What other verses come to mind as you read these passages?

What questions do you still have? What do you want to know more about? What lesson or theme are you picking up on?

How can you apply these scriptures to your life? -

Today's prayers:

All Access Pass — Day 260

What verse spoke to you in this reading?

Do the New Testament and Old Testament passages have any similarities?

What other verses come to mind as you read these passages?

What questions do you still have? What do you want to know more about? What lesson or theme are you picking up on?

How can you apply these scriptures to your life? -

Today's prayers:

Today's passages:

Isaiah 25:1-28:13

Galatians 3:10-22

Psalm 61:1-8

Proverbs 23:17-18

Notes

All Access Pass — Day 261

Today's passages:

Isaiah 28:14-30:11

Galatians 3:23-4:31

Psalm 62:1-12

Proverbs 23:19-21

Notes

What verse spoke to you in this reading?

Do the New Testament and Old Testament passages have any similarities?

What other verses come to mind as you read these passages?

What questions do you still have? What do you want to know more about? What lesson or theme are you picking up on?

How can you apply these scriptures to your life? -

Today's prayers:

All Access Pass — Day 262

Today's passages:

Isaiah 30:12-33:9

Galatians 5:1-12

Psalm 63:1-11

Proverbs 23:22

Notes

What verse spoke to you in this reading?

Do the New Testament and Old Testament passages have any similarities?

What other verses come to mind as you read these passages?

What questions do you still have? What do you want to know more about? What lesson or theme are you picking up on?

How can you apply these scriptures to your life? -

Today's prayers:

All Access Pass — Day 263

Today's passages:

Isaiah 33:10-36:22

Galatians 5:13-26

Psalm 64:1-10

Proverbs 23:23

Notes

What verse spoke to you in this reading?

Do the New Testament and Old Testament passages have any similarities?

What other verses come to mind as you read these passages?

What questions do you still have? What do you want to know more about? What lesson or theme are you picking up on?

How can you apply these scriptures to your life? -

Today's prayers:

All Access Pass — Day 264

Today's passages:

Isaiah 37:1-38:22

Galatians 6:1-18

Psalm 65:1-13

Proverbs 23:24

Notes

What verse spoke to you in this reading?

Do the New Testament and Old Testament passages have any similarities?

What other verses come to mind as you read these passages?

What questions do you still have? What do you want to know more about? What lesson or theme are you picking up on?

How can you apply these scriptures to your life? -

Today's prayers:

All Access Pass — Day 265

Today's passages:

Isaiah 39:1-41:16

Ephesians 1:1-23

Psalm 66:1-20

Proverbs 23:25-28

Notes

What verse spoke to you in this reading?

Do the New Testament and Old Testament passages have any similarities?

What other verses come to mind as you read these passages?

What questions do you still have? What do you want to know more about? What lesson or theme are you picking up on?

How can you apply these scriptures to your life? -

Today's prayers:

All Access Pass — Day 266

Today's passages:

Isaiah 41:17-43:13

Ephesians 2:1-22

Psalm 67;1-7

Proverbs 23:29-35

Notes

What verse spoke to you in this reading?

Do the New Testament and Old Testament passages have any similarities?

What other verses come to mind as you read these passages?

What questions do you still have? What do you want to know more about? What lesson or theme are you picking up on?

How can you apply these scriptures to your life? -

Today's prayers:

All Access Pass — Day 267

Today's passages:

Isaiah 43:14-45:10

Ephesians 3:1-21

Psalm 68:1-18

Proverbs 24:1-2

Notes

What verse spoke to you in this reading?

Do the New Testament and Old Testament passages have any similarities?

What other verses come to mind as you read these passages?

What questions do you still have? What do you want to know more about? What lesson or theme are you picking up on?

How can you apply these scriptures to your life? -

Today's prayers:

All Access Pass — Day 268

Today's passages:

Isaiah 45;11-48:11

Ephesians 4:1-16

Psalm 68:19-35

Proverbs 24:3-4

Notes

What verse spoke to you in this reading?

Do the New Testament and Old Testament passages have any similarities?

What other verses come to mind as you read these passages?

What questions do you still have? What do you want to know more about? What lesson or theme are you picking up on?

How can you apply these scriptures to your life? -

Today's prayers:

All Access Pass — Day 269

Today's passages:

Isaiah 48:12-50:11

Ephesians 4:17-32

Psalm 69:1-18

Proverbs 24:5-6

Notes

What verse spoke to you in this reading?

Do the New Testament and Old Testament passages have any similarities?

What other verses come to mind as you read these passages?

What questions do you still have? What do you want to know more about? What lesson or theme are you picking up on?

How can you apply these scriptures to your life? -

Today's prayers:

All Access Pass — Day 270

What verse spoke to you in this reading?

Do the New Testament and Old Testament passages have any similarities?

What other verses come to mind as you read these passages?

What questions do you still have? What do you want to know more about? What lesson or theme are you picking up on?

How can you apply these scriptures to your life? -

Today's prayers:

Today's passages:

Isaiah 51:1-53:12

Ephesians 5:1-33

Psalm 69:19-36

Proverbs 24:7

Notes

All Access Pass — Day 271

Today's passages:

Isaiah 54:1-57:14

Ephesians 6:1-24

Psalm 70:1-5

Proverbs 24:8

Notes

What verse spoke to you in this reading?

Do the New Testament and Old Testament passages have any similarities?

What other verses come to mind as you read these passages?

What questions do you still have? What do you want to know more about? What lesson or theme are you picking up on?

How can you apply these scriptures to your life? -

Today's prayers:

All Access Pass — Day 272

Today's passages:

Isaiah 57:15-59:21

Philippians 1:1-26

Psalm 71:1-24

Proverbs 24:9-10

Notes

What verse spoke to you in this reading?

Do the New Testament and Old Testament passages have any similarities?

What other verses come to mind as you read these passages?

What questions do you still have? What do you want to know more about? What lesson or theme are you picking up on?

How can you apply these scriptures to your life? -

Today's prayers:

All Access Pass — Day 273

Today's passages:

Isaiah 60:1-62:5

Philippians 1:27-2:18

Psalm 72:1-20

Proverbs 24:11-12

What verse spoke to you in this reading?

Do the New Testament and Old Testament passages have any similarities?

What other verses come to mind as you read these passages?

What questions do you still have? What do you want to know more about? What lesson or theme are you picking up on?

How can you apply these scriptures to your life? -

Today's prayers:

All Access Pass — Day 274

Today's passages:

Isaiah 62:6-65:25

Philippians 2:19-3:3

Psalm 73:1-28

Proverbs 24:13-14

Notes

What verse spoke to you in this reading?

Do the New Testament and Old Testament passages have any similarities?

What other verses come to mind as you read these passages?

What questions do you still have? What do you want to know more about? What lesson or theme are you picking up on?

How can you apply these scriptures to your life? -

Today's prayers:

All Access Pass — Day 275

Today's passages:

Isaiah 66:1-24

Philippians 3:4-21

Psalm 74:1-23

Proverbs 24:15-16

Notes

What verse spoke to you in this reading?

Do the New Testament and Old Testament passages have any similarities?

What other verses come to mind as you read these passages?

What questions do you still have? What do you want to know more about? What lesson or theme are you picking up on?

How can you apply these scriptures to your life? -

Today's prayers:

All Access Pass — Day 276

Today's passages:

Jeremiah 1:1-2:30

Philippians 4:1-23

Psalm 75:1-10

Proverbs 24:17-20

Notes

What verse spoke to you in this reading?

Do the New Testament and Old Testament passages have any similarities?

What other verses come to mind as you read these passages?

What questions do you still have? What do you want to know more about? What lesson or theme are you picking up on?

How can you apply these scriptures to your life? -

Today's prayers:

All Access Pass — Day 277

Today's passages:

Jeremiah 2:31-4:18

Colossians 1:1-17

Psalm 76:1-12

Proverbs 24:21-22

Notes

What verse spoke to you in this reading?

Do the New Testament and Old Testament passages have any similarities?

What other verses come to mind as you read these passages?

What questions do you still have? What do you want to know more about? What lesson or theme are you picking up on?

How can you apply these scriptures to your life? -

Today's prayers:

All Access Pass — Day 278

Today's passages:

Jeremiah 4:19-6:15

Colossians 1:18-2:7

Psalm 77:1-20

Proverbs 24:23-25

Notes

What verse spoke to you in this reading?

Do the New Testament and Old Testament passages have any similarities?

What other verses come to mind as you read these passages?

What questions do you still have? What do you want to know more about? What lesson or theme are you picking up on?

How can you apply these scriptures to your life? -

Today's prayers:

All Access Pass — Day 279

Today's passages:

Jeremiah 6:16-8:7

Colossians 2:8-23

Psalm 78:1-31

Proverbs 24:26

Notes

What verse spoke to you in this reading?

Do the New Testament and Old Testament passages have any similarities?

What other verses come to mind as you read these passages?

What questions do you still have? What do you want to know more about? What lesson or theme are you picking up on?

How can you apply these scriptures to your life? -

Today's prayers:

 **Day 280**

What verse spoke to you in this reading?

Do the New Testament and Old Testament passages have any similarities?

What other verses come to mind as you read these passages?

What questions do you still have? What do you want to know more about? What lesson or theme are you picking up on?

How can you apply these scriptures to your life? -

Today's prayers:

Today's passages:

Jeremiah 8:8-9:26

Colossians 3:1-17

Psalm 78:32-55

Proverbs 24:27

All Access Pass — Day 281

Today's passages:

Jeremiah 10:1-11:23

Colossians 3:18-4:18

Psalm 78:56-72

Proverbs 24:28-29

Notes

What verse spoke to you in this reading?

Do the New Testament and Old Testament passages have any similarities?

What other verses come to mind as you read these passages?

What questions do you still have? What do you want to know more about? What lesson or theme are you picking up on?

How can you apply these scriptures to your life? -

Today's prayers:

All Access Pass — Day 282

What verse spoke to you in this reading?

Do the New Testament and Old Testament passages have any similarities?

What other verses come to mind as you read these passages?

What questions do you still have? What do you want to know more about? What lesson or theme are you picking up on?

How can you apply these scriptures to your life? -

Today's prayers:

Today's passages:

Jeremiah 12:1-14:10

1 Thessalonians 1:1-2:8

Psalm 79:1-13

Proverbs 24:30-34

Notes

All Access Pass — Day 283

Today's passages:

Jeremiah 14:11-16:15

1 Thessalonians 2:9-3:13

Psalm 80:1-19

Proverbs 25:1-5

What verse spoke to you in this reading?

Do the New Testament and Old Testament passages have any similarities?

What other verses come to mind as you read these passages?

What questions do you still have? What do you want to know more about? What lesson or theme are you picking up on?

How can you apply these scriptures to your life? -

Today's prayers:

All Access Pass — Day 284

Today's passages:

Jeremiah 16:16-18:23

1 Thessalonians 4:1-5:3

Psalm 81:1-16

Proverbs 25:6-8

Notes

What verse spoke to you in this reading?

Do the New Testament and Old Testament passages have any similarities?

What other verses come to mind as you read these passages?

What questions do you still have? What do you want to know more about? What lesson or theme are you picking up on?

How can you apply these scriptures to your life? -

Today's prayers:

All Access Pass — Day 285

Today's passages:

Jeremiah 19:1-21:14

1 Thessalonians 5:4-28

Psalm 82:1-8

Proverbs 25:9-10

Notes

What verse spoke to you in this reading?

Do the New Testament and Old Testament passages have any similarities?

What other verses come to mind as you read these passages?

What questions do you still have? What do you want to know more about? What lesson or theme are you picking up on?

How can you apply these scriptures to your life? -

Today's prayers:

All Access Pass — Day 286

Today's passages:

Jeremiah 22:1-23:20

2 Thessalonians 1:1-12

Psalm 83:1-18

Proverbs 25:11-14

Notes

What verse spoke to you in this reading?

Do the New Testament and Old Testament passages have any similarities?

What other verses come to mind as you read these passages?

What questions do you still have? What do you want to know more about? What lesson or theme are you picking up on?

How can you apply these scriptures to your life? -

Today's prayers:

All Access Pass — Day 287

Today's passages:

Jeremiah 23:21-25:38

2 Thessalonians 2:1-17

Psalm 84:1-12

Proverbs 25:15

Notes

What verse spoke to you in this reading?

Do the New Testament and Old Testament passages have any similarities?

What other verses come to mind as you read these passages?

What questions do you still have? What do you want to know more about? What lesson or theme are you picking up on?

How can you apply these scriptures to your life? -

Today's prayers:

All Access Pass — Day 288

Today's passages:

Jeremiah 26:1-27

2 Thessalonians 3:1-18

Psalm 85:1-13

Proverbs 25:16

Notes

What verse spoke to you in this reading?

Do the New Testament and Old Testament passages have any similarities?

What other verses come to mind as you read these passages?

What questions do you still have? What do you want to know more about? What lesson or theme are you picking up on?

How can you apply these scriptures to your life? -

Today's prayers:

All Access Pass — Day 289

Today's passages:

Jeremiah 28:1-29:32

1 Timothy 1:1-20

Psalm 86:1-17

Proverbs 25:17

Notes

What verse spoke to you in this reading?

Do the New Testament and Old Testament passages have any similarities?

What other verses come to mind as you read these passages?

What questions do you still have? What do you want to know more about? What lesson or theme are you picking up on?

How can you apply these scriptures to your life? -

Today's prayers:

All Access Pass — Day 290

What verse spoke to you in this reading?

Do the New Testament and Old Testament passages have any similarities?

What other verses come to mind as you read these passages?

What questions do you still have? What do you want to know more about? What lesson or theme are you picking up on?

How can you apply these scriptures to your life? -

Today's prayers:

Today's passages:

Jeremiah 30:1-31:26

1 Timothy 2:1-15

Psalm 87:1-7

Proverbs 25:18-19

Notes

All Access Pass — Day 291

Today's passages:

Jeremiah 31:27-32:44

1 Timothy 3:1-16

Psalm 88:1-18

Proverbs 25:20-22

Notes

What verse spoke to you in this reading?

Do the New Testament and Old Testament passages have any similarities?

What other verses come to mind as you read these passages?

What questions do you still have? What do you want to know more about? What lesson or theme are you picking up on?

How can you apply these scriptures to your life? -

Today's prayers:

All Access Pass — Day 292

Today's passages:

Jeremiah 33:1-34:22

1 Timothy 4:1-16

Psalm 89:1-13

Proverbs 25:23-24

Notes

What verse spoke to you in this reading?

Do the New Testament and Old Testament passages have any similarities?

What other verses come to mind as you read these passages?

What questions do you still have? What do you want to know more about? What lesson or theme are you picking up on?

How can you apply these scriptures to your life? -

Today's prayers:

All Access Pass — Day 293

Today's passages:

Jeremiah 35:1-36:32

1 Timothy 5:1-25

Psalm 89:14-37

Proverbs 25:25-27

Notes

What verse spoke to you in this reading?

Do the New Testament and Old Testament passages have any similarities?

What other verses come to mind as you read these passages?

What questions do you still have? What do you want to know more about? What lesson or theme are you picking up on?

How can you apply these scriptures to your life? -

Today's prayers:

All Access Pass — Day 294

What verse spoke to you in this reading?

Do the New Testament and Old Testament passages have any similarities?

What other verses come to mind as you read these passages?

What questions do you still have? What do you want to know more about? What lesson or theme are you picking up on?

How can you apply these scriptures to your life? -

Today's prayers:

Today's passages:

Jeremiah 37:1-38:28

1 Timothy 6:1-21

Psalm 89:38-52

Proverbs 25:28

Notes

All Access Pass — Day 295

Today's passages:

Jeremiah 39:1-41:18

2 Timothy 1:1-18

Psalm 90:1-91:16

Proverbs 26:1-2

Notes

What verse spoke to you in this reading?

Do the New Testament and Old Testament passages have any similarities?

What other verses come to mind as you read these passages?

What questions do you still have? What do you want to know more about? What lesson or theme are you picking up on?

How can you apply these scriptures to your life? -

Today's prayers:

All Access Pass — Day 296

Today's passages:

Jeremiah 42:1-44:23

2 Timothy 2:1-21

Psalm 92:1-93

Proverbs 26:3-5

Notes

What verse spoke to you in this reading?

Do the New Testament and Old Testament passages have any similarities?

What other verses come to mind as you read these passages?

What questions do you still have? What do you want to know more about? What lesson or theme are you picking up on?

How can you apply these scriptures to your life? -

Today's prayers:

All Access Pass — Day 297

Today's passages:

Jeremiah 44:24-47:7

2 Timothy 2:22-3:17

Psalm 94:1-23

Proverbs 26:6-8

Notes

What verse spoke to you in this reading?

Do the New Testament and Old Testament passages have any similarities?

What other verses come to mind as you read these passages?

What questions do you still have? What do you want to know more about? What lesson or theme are you picking up on?

How can you apply these scriptures to your life? -

Today's prayers:

All Access Pass — Day 298

What verse spoke to you in this reading?

Do the New Testament and Old Testament passages have any similarities?

What other verses come to mind as you read these passages?

What questions do you still have? What do you want to know more about? What lesson or theme are you picking up on?

How can you apply these scriptures to your life? -

Today's prayers:

Today's passages:

Jeremiah 48:1-49:22

2 Timothy 4:1-22

Psalm 95:1-96:13

Proverbs 26:9-12

Notes

All Access Pass — Day 299

Today's passages:

Jeremiah 49:23-50:46

Titus 1:1-16

Psalm 97:1-98:9

Proverbs 26:13-16

Notes

What verse spoke to you in this reading?

Do the New Testament and Old Testament passages have any similarities?

What other verses come to mind as you read these passages?

What questions do you still have? What do you want to know more about? What lesson or theme are you picking up on?

How can you apply these scriptures to your life? -

Today's prayers:

All Access Pass — Day 300

What verse spoke to you in this reading?

Do the New Testament and Old Testament passages have any similarities?

What other verses come to mind as you read these passages?

What questions do you still have? What do you want to know more about? What lesson or theme are you picking up on?

How can you apply these scriptures to your life? -

Today's prayers:

Today's passages:

Jeremiah 51:1-53

Titus 2:1-15

Psalm 99:1-9

Proverbs 26:17

Notes

All Access Pass — Day 301

Today's passages:

Jeremiah 51:54-52:34

Titus 3:1-15

Psalm 100:1-5

Proverbs 26:18-19

Notes

What verse spoke to you in this reading?

Do the New Testament and Old Testament passages have any similarities?

What other verses come to mind as you read these passages?

What questions do you still have? What do you want to know more about? What lesson or theme are you picking up on?

How can you apply these scriptures to your life? -

Today's prayers:

All Access Pass — Day 302

Today's passages:

Lamentations 1:1-2:22

Philemon 1:1-25

Psalm 101:1-8

Proverbs 26:20

Notes

What verse spoke to you in this reading?

Do the New Testament and Old Testament passages have any similarities?

What other verses come to mind as you read these passages?

What questions do you still have? What do you want to know more about? What lesson or theme are you picking up on?

How can you apply these scriptures to your life? -

Today's prayers:

All Access Pass — Day 303

Today's passages:

Lamentations 3:1-66

Hebrews 1:1-14

Psalm 102:1-28

Proverbs 26:21-22

What verse spoke to you in this reading?

Do the New Testament and Old Testament passages have any similarities?

What other verses come to mind as you read these passages?

What questions do you still have? What do you want to know more about? What lesson or theme are you picking up on?

How can you apply these scriptures to your life? -

Today's prayers:

All Access Pass — Day 304

Today's passages:

Lamentations 4:1-5:22

Hebrews 2:1-18

Psalm 103:1-22

Proverbs 26:23

Notes

What verse spoke to you in this reading?

Do the New Testament and Old Testament passages have any similarities?

What other verses come to mind as you read these passages?

What questions do you still have? What do you want to know more about? What lesson or theme are you picking up on?

How can you apply these scriptures to your life? -

Today's prayers:

All Access Pass — Day 305

Today's passages:

Ezekiel 1:1-3:15

Hebrews 3:1-19

Psalm 104:1-23

Proverbs 26:24-26

Notes

What verse spoke to you in this reading?

Do the New Testament and Old Testament passages have any similarities?

What other verses come to mind as you read these passages?

What questions do you still have? What do you want to know more about? What lesson or theme are you picking up on?

How can you apply these scriptures to your life? -

Today's prayers:

All Access Pass — Day 306

Today's passages:

Ezekiel 3:16-6:14

Hebrews 4:1-16

Psalm 104:24-35

Proverbs 26:27

Notes

What verse spoke to you in this reading?

Do the New Testament and Old Testament passages have any similarities?

What other verses come to mind as you read these passages?

What questions do you still have? What do you want to know more about? What lesson or theme are you picking up on?

How can you apply these scriptures to your life? -

Today's prayers:

All Access Pass — Day 307

Today's passages:

Ezekiel 7:1-9:11

Hebrews 5:1-14

Psalm 105:1-15

Proverbs 26:28

Notes

What verse spoke to you in this reading?

Do the New Testament and Old Testament passages have any similarities?

What other verses come to mind as you read these passages?

What questions do you still have? What do you want to know more about? What lesson or theme are you picking up on?

How can you apply these scriptures to your life? -

Today's prayers:

All Access Pass — Day 308

Today's passages:

Ezekiel 10:1-11:25

Hebrews 6:1-20

Psalm 105:16-36

Proverbs 27:1-2

What verse spoke to you in this reading?

Do the New Testament and Old Testament passages have any similarities?

What other verses come to mind as you read these passages?

What questions do you still have? What do you want to know more about? What lesson or theme are you picking up on?

How can you apply these scriptures to your life? -

Today's prayers:

All Access Pass — Day 309

Today's passages:

Ezekiel 12:1-14:11

Hebrews 7:1-17

Psalm 105:37-45

Proverbs 27:3

Notes

What verse spoke to you in this reading?

Do the New Testament and Old Testament passages have any similarities?

What other verses come to mind as you read these passages?

What questions do you still have? What do you want to know more about? What lesson or theme are you picking up on?

How can you apply these scriptures to your life? -

Today's prayers:

All Access Pass — Day 310

Today's passages:

Ezekiel 14:12-16:41

Hebrews 7:18-28

Psalm 106:1-12

Proverbs 27:4-6

Notes

What verse spoke to you in this reading?

Do the New Testament and Old Testament passages have any similarities?

What other verses come to mind as you read these passages?

What questions do you still have? What do you want to know more about? What lesson or theme are you picking up on?

How can you apply these scriptures to your life? -

Today's prayers:

All Access Pass

Today's passages:

Ezekiel 16:42-17:24

Hebrews 8:1-13

Psalm 106:13-31

Proverbs 27:7-9

What verse spoke to you in this reading?

Do the New Testament and Old Testament passages have any similarities?

What other verses come to mind as you read these passages?

What questions do you still have? What do you want to know more about? What lesson or theme are you picking up on?

How can you apply these scriptures to your life? -

Today's prayers:

All Access Pass — Day 312

Today's passages:

Ezekiel 18:1-19:14

Hebrews 9:1-10

Psalm 106:32-48

Proverbs 27:10

Notes

What verse spoke to you in this reading?

Do the New Testament and Old Testament passages have any similarities?

What other verses come to mind as you read these passages?

What questions do you still have? What do you want to know more about? What lesson or theme are you picking up on?

How can you apply these scriptures to your life? -

Today's prayers:

All Access Pass — Day 313

Today's passages:

Ezekiel 20:1-49

Hebrews 9:11-28

Psalm 107:1-43

Proverbs 27:11

Notes

What verse spoke to you in this reading?

Do the New Testament and Old Testament passages have any similarities?

What other verses come to mind as you read these passages?

What questions do you still have? What do you want to know more about? What lesson or theme are you picking up on?

How can you apply these scriptures to your life? -

Today's prayers:

All Access Pass — Day 314

Today's passages:

Ezekiel 21:1-22:31

Hebrews 10:1-17

Psalm 108:1-13

Proverbs 27:12

Notes

What verse spoke to you in this reading?

Do the New Testament and Old Testament passages have any similarities?

What other verses come to mind as you read these passages?

What questions do you still have? What do you want to know more about? What lesson or theme are you picking up on?

How can you apply these scriptures to your life? -

Today's prayers:

All Access Pass — Day 315

Today's passages:

Ezekiel 23:1-49

Hebrews 10:18-39

Psalm 109:1-31

Proverbs 27:13

What verse spoke to you in this reading?

Do the New Testament and Old Testament passages have any similarities?

What other verses come to mind as you read these passages?

What questions do you still have? What do you want to know more about? What lesson or theme are you picking up on?

How can you apply these scriptures to your life? -

Today's prayers:

All Access Pass — Day 316

Today's passages:

Ezekiel 24:1-26:21

Hebrews 11:1-16

Psalm 110:1-7

Proverbs 27:14

Notes

What verse spoke to you in this reading?

Do the New Testament and Old Testament passages have any similarities?

What other verses come to mind as you read these passages?

What questions do you still have? What do you want to know more about? What lesson or theme are you picking up on?

How can you apply these scriptures to your life? -

Today's prayers:

All Access Pass — Day 317

Today's passages:

Ezekiel 27:1-28:26

Hebrews 11:17-31

Psalm 111:1-10

Proverbs 27:15-16

Notes

What verse spoke to you in this reading?

Do the New Testament and Old Testament passages have any similarities?

What other verses come to mind as you read these passages?

What questions do you still have? What do you want to know more about? What lesson or theme are you picking up on?

How can you apply these scriptures to your life? -

Today's prayers:

All Access Pass — Day 318

Today's passages:

Ezekiel 29:1-30:26

Hebrews 11:32-12:13

Psalm 112:1-10

Proverbs 27:17

Notes

What verse spoke to you in this reading?

Do the New Testament and Old Testament passages have any similarities?

What other verses come to mind as you read these passages?

What questions do you still have? What do you want to know more about? What lesson or theme are you picking up on?

How can you apply these scriptures to your life? -

Today's prayers:

All Access Pass — Day 319

Today's passages:

Ezekiel 31:1-32:32

Hebrews 12:14-29

Psalm 113:1-114:8

Proverbs 27:18-20

Notes

What verse spoke to you in this reading?

Do the New Testament and Old Testament passages have any similarities?

What other verses come to mind as you read these passages?

What questions do you still have? What do you want to know more about? What lesson or theme are you picking up on?

How can you apply these scriptures to your life? -

Today's prayers:

All Access Pass — Day 320

Today's passages:

Ezekiel 33:1-34:31

Hebrews 13:1-25

Psalm 115:1-18

Proverbs 27:21-22

Notes

What verse spoke to you in this reading?

Do the New Testament and Old Testament passages have any similarities?

What other verses come to mind as you read these passages?

What questions do you still have? What do you want to know more about? What lesson or theme are you picking up on?

How can you apply these scriptures to your life? -

Today's prayers:

All Access Pass — Day 321

Today's passages:

Ezekiel 35:1-36:38

James 1:1-18

Psalm 116:1-19

Proverbs 27:23-27

Notes

What verse spoke to you in this reading?

Do the New Testament and Old Testament passages have any similarities?

What other verses come to mind as you read these passages?

What questions do you still have? What do you want to know more about? What lesson or theme are you picking up on?

How can you apply these scriptures to your life? -

Today's prayers:

All Access Pass — Day 322

Today's passages:

Ezekiel 37:1-38:23

James 1:19-2:17

Psalm 117:1-2

Proverbs 28:1

Notes

What verse spoke to you in this reading?

Do the New Testament and Old Testament passages have any similarities?

What other verses come to mind as you read these passages?

What questions do you still have? What do you want to know more about? What lesson or theme are you picking up on?

How can you apply these scriptures to your life? -

Today's prayers:

All Access Pass — Day 323

Today's passages:

Ezekiel 39:1-40:27

James 2:18-3:18

Psalm 118:1-18

Proverbs 28:2

Notes

What verse spoke to you in this reading?

Do the New Testament and Old Testament passages have any similarities?

What other verses come to mind as you read these passages?

What questions do you still have? What do you want to know more about? What lesson or theme are you picking up on?

How can you apply these scriptures to your life? -

Today's prayers:

All Access Pass — Day 324

Today's passages:

Ezekiel 40:28-41:26

James 4:1-17

Psalm 118:19-29

Proverbs 28:3-5

Notes

What verse spoke to you in this reading?

Do the New Testament and Old Testament passages have any similarities?

What other verses come to mind as you read these passages?

What questions do you still have? What do you want to know more about? What lesson or theme are you picking up on?

How can you apply these scriptures to your life? -

Today's prayers:

All Access Pass — Day 325

Today's passages:

Ezekiel 42:1-43:27

James 5:1-20

Psalm 119:1-16

Proverbs 28:6-7

Notes

What verse spoke to you in this reading?

Do the New Testament and Old Testament passages have any similarities?

What other verses come to mind as you read these passages?

What questions do you still have? What do you want to know more about? What lesson or theme are you picking up on?

How can you apply these scriptures to your life? -

Today's prayers:

All Access Pass — Day 326

Today's passages:

Ezekiel 44:1-45:12

1 Peter 1:1-12

Psalm 119:17-32

Proverbs 28:8-10

Notes

What verse spoke to you in this reading?

Do the New Testament and Old Testament passages have any similarities?

What other verses come to mind as you read these passages?

What questions do you still have? What do you want to know more about? What lesson or theme are you picking up on?

How can you apply these scriptures to your life? -

Today's prayers:

All Access Pass — Day 327

Today's passages:

Ezekiel 45:13-46:24

1 Peter 1:13-2:10

Psalm 119:33-48

Proverbs 28:11

Notes

What verse spoke to you in this reading?

Do the New Testament and Old Testament passages have any similarities?

What other verses come to mind as you read these passages?

What questions do you still have? What do you want to know more about? What lesson or theme are you picking up on?

How can you apply these scriptures to your life? -

Today's prayers:

All Access Pass — Day 328

Today's passages:

Ezekiel 47:1-48:35

1 Peter 2:11-3:7

Psalm 119:49-64

Proverbs 28:12-13

What verse spoke to you in this reading?

Do the New Testament and Old Testament passages have any similarities?

What other verses come to mind as you read these passages?

What questions do you still have? What do you want to know more about? What lesson or theme are you picking up on?

How can you apply these scriptures to your life? -

Today's prayers:

All Access Pass — Day 329

Today's passages:

Daniel 1:1-2:23

1 Peter 3:8-4:6

Psalm 119:65-80

Proverbs 28:14

Notes

What verse spoke to you in this reading?

Do the New Testament and Old Testament passages have any similarities?

What other verses come to mind as you read these passages?

What questions do you still have? What do you want to know more about? What lesson or theme are you picking up on?

How can you apply these scriptures to your life? -

Today's prayers:

All Access Pass — Day 330

Today's passages:

Daniel 2:24-3:30

1 Peter 4:7-5:14

Psalm 119:81-96

Proverbs 28:15-16

Notes

What verse spoke to you in this reading?

Do the New Testament and Old Testament passages have any similarities?

What other verses come to mind as you read these passages?

What questions do you still have? What do you want to know more about? What lesson or theme are you picking up on?

How can you apply these scriptures to your life? -

Today's prayers:

All Access Pass — Day 331

Today's passages:

Daniel 4:1-37

2 Peter 1:1-21

Psalm 119:97-112

Proverbs 28:17-18

What verse spoke to you in this reading?

Do the New Testament and Old Testament passages have any similarities?

What other verses come to mind as you read these passages?

What questions do you still have? What do you want to know more about? What lesson or theme are you picking up on?

How can you apply these scriptures to your life? -

Today's prayers:

 Day 332

What verse spoke to you in this reading?

Do the New Testament and Old Testament passages have any similarities?

What other verses come to mind as you read these passages?

What questions do you still have? What do you want to know more about? What lesson or theme are you picking up on?

How can you apply these scriptures to your life? -

Today's prayers:

Today's passages:

Daniel 5:1-31

2 Peter 2:1-22

Psalm 119:113-128

Proverbs 28:19-20

All Access Pass — Day 333

Today's passages:

Daniel 6:1-28

2 Peter 3:1-18

Psalm 119:129-152

Proverbs 28:21-22

What verse spoke to you in this reading?

Do the New Testament and Old Testament passages have any similarities?

What other verses come to mind as you read these passages?

What questions do you still have? What do you want to know more about? What lesson or theme are you picking up on?

How can you apply these scriptures to your life? -

Today's prayers:

All Access Pass — Day 334

What verse spoke to you in this reading?

Do the New Testament and Old Testament passages have any similarities?

What other verses come to mind as you read these passages?

What questions do you still have? What do you want to know more about? What lesson or theme are you picking up on?

How can you apply these scriptures to your life? -

Today's prayers:

Today's passages:

Daniel 7:1-28

1 John 1:1-10

Psalm 119:153-176

Proverbs 28:23-24

Notes

All Access Pass Day 335

Today's passages:

Daniel 8:1-27

1 John 2:1-17

Psalm 120:1-7

Proverbs 28:25-26

What verse spoke to you in this reading?

Do the New Testament and Old Testament passages have any similarities?

What other verses come to mind as you read these passages?

What questions do you still have? What do you want to know more about? What lesson or theme are you picking up on?

How can you apply these scriptures to your life? -

Today's prayers:

All Access Pass — Day 336

Today's passages:

Daniel 9:1-11:1

1 John 2:18-3:6

Psalm 121:1-8

Proverbs 28:27-28

Notes

What verse spoke to you in this reading?

Do the New Testament and Old Testament passages have any similarities?

What other verses come to mind as you read these passages?

What questions do you still have? What do you want to know more about? What lesson or theme are you picking up on?

How can you apply these scriptures to your life? -

Today's prayers:

All Access Pass — Day 337

Today's passages:

Daniel 11:2-35

1 John 3:7-24

Psalm 122:1-9

Proverbs 29:1

Notes

What verse spoke to you in this reading?

Do the New Testament and Old Testament passages have any similarities?

What other verses come to mind as you read these passages?

What questions do you still have? What do you want to know more about? What lesson or theme are you picking up on?

How can you apply these scriptures to your life? -

Today's prayers:

All Access Pass — Day 338

Today's passages:

Daniel 11:36-12:13

1 John 4:1-21

Psalm 123:1-4

Proverbs 29:2-4

What verse spoke to you in this reading?

Do the New Testament and Old Testament passages have any similarities?

What other verses come to mind as you read these passages?

What questions do you still have? What do you want to know more about? What lesson or theme are you picking up on?

How can you apply these scriptures to your life? -

Today's prayers:

All Access Pass — Day 339

Today's passages:

Hosea 1:1-3:5

1 John 5:1-21

Psalm 124:1-8

Proverbs 29:5-8

Notes

What verse spoke to you in this reading?

Do the New Testament and Old Testament passages have any similarities?

What other verses come to mind as you read these passages?

What questions do you still have? What do you want to know more about? What lesson or theme are you picking up on?

How can you apply these scriptures to your life? -

Today's prayers:

All Access Pass — Day 340

Today's passages:

Hosea 4:1-5:15

2 John 1:1-13

Psalm 125:1-5

Proverbs 29:9-11

Notes

What verse spoke to you in this reading?

Do the New Testament and Old Testament passages have any similarities?

What other verses come to mind as you read these passages?

What questions do you still have? What do you want to know more about? What lesson or theme are you picking up on?

How can you apply these scriptures to your life? -

Today's prayers:

All Access Pass — Day 341

Today's passages:

Hosea 6:1-9:17

3 John 1:1-15

Psalm 126:1-6

Proverbs 29:12-14

Notes

What verse spoke to you in this reading?

Do the New Testament and Old Testament passages have any similarities?

What other verses come to mind as you read these passages?

What questions do you still have? What do you want to know more about? What lesson or theme are you picking up on?

How can you apply these scriptures to your life? -

Today's prayers:

All Access Pass — Day 342

Today's passages:

Hosea 10:1-14:9

Jude 1:1-25

Psalm 127:1-5

Proverbs 29:15-17

Notes

What verse spoke to you in this reading?

Do the New Testament and Old Testament passages have any similarities?

What other verses come to mind as you read these passages?

What questions do you still have? What do you want to know more about? What lesson or theme are you picking up on?

How can you apply these scriptures to your life? -

Today's prayers:

All Access Pass — Day 343

Today's passages:

Joel 1:1-3:21

Revelation 1:1-20

Psalm 128:1-6

Proverbs 29:18

Notes

What verse spoke to you in this reading?

Do the New Testament and Old Testament passages have any similarities?

What other verses come to mind as you read these passages?

What questions do you still have? What do you want to know more about? What lesson or theme are you picking up on?

How can you apply these scriptures to your life? -

Today's prayers:

All Access Pass — Day 344

Today's passages:

Amos 1:1-3:15

Revelation 2:1-17

Psalm 129:1-8

Proverbs 29:19-20

Notes

What verse spoke to you in this reading?

Do the New Testament and Old Testament passages have any similarities?

What other verses come to mind as you read these passages?

What questions do you still have? What do you want to know more about? What lesson or theme are you picking up on?

How can you apply these scriptures to your life? -

Today's prayers:

All Access Pass — Day 345

Today's passages:

Amos 4:1-6:14

Revelation 2:18-3:6

Psalm 130:1-8

Proverbs 29:21-22

Notes

What verse spoke to you in this reading?

Do the New Testament and Old Testament passages have any similarities?

What other verses come to mind as you read these passages?

What questions do you still have? What do you want to know more about? What lesson or theme are you picking up on?

How can you apply these scriptures to your life? -

Today's prayers:

All Access Pass — Day 346

Today's passages:

Amos 7:1-9:15

Revelation 3:7-22

Psalm 131:1-3

Proverbs 29:23

Notes

What verse spoke to you in this reading?

Do the New Testament and Old Testament passages have any similarities?

What other verses come to mind as you read these passages?

What questions do you still have? What do you want to know more about? What lesson or theme are you picking up on?

How can you apply these scriptures to your life? -

Today's prayers:

All Access Pass — Day 347

Today's passages:

Obadiah 1:1-21

Revelation 4:1-11

Psalm 132:1-18

Proverbs 29:24-25

Notes

What verse spoke to you in this reading?

Do the New Testament and Old Testament passages have any similarities?

What other verses come to mind as you read these passages?

What questions do you still have? What do you want to know more about? What lesson or theme are you picking up on?

How can you apply these scriptures to your life? -

Today's prayers:

All Access Pass — Day 348

Today's passages:

Jonah 1:1-4:11

Revelation 5:1-14

Psalm 133:1-3

Proverbs 29:26-27

Notes

What verse spoke to you in this reading?

Do the New Testament and Old Testament passages have any similarities?

What other verses come to mind as you read these passages?

What questions do you still have? What do you want to know more about? What lesson or theme are you picking up on?

How can you apply these scriptures to your life? -

Today's prayers:

All Access Pass — Day 349

Today's passages:

Micah 1:1-4:13

Revelation 6:1-17

Psalm 134:1-3

Proverbs 30:1-4

Notes

What verse spoke to you in this reading?

Do the New Testament and Old Testament passages have any similarities?

What other verses come to mind as you read these passages?

What questions do you still have? What do you want to know more about? What lesson or theme are you picking up on?

How can you apply these scriptures to your life? -

Today's prayers:

All Access Pass — Day 350

Today's passages:

Micah 5:1-7:20

Revelation 7:1-17

Psalm 135:1-21

Proverbs 30:5-6

Notes

What verse spoke to you in this reading?

Do the New Testament and Old Testament passages have any similarities?

What other verses come to mind as you read these passages?

What questions do you still have? What do you want to know more about? What lesson or theme are you picking up on?

How can you apply these scriptures to your life? -

Today's prayers:

All Access Pass — Day 351

Today's passages:

Nahum 1:1-3:19

Revelation 8:1-13

Psalm 136:1-26

Proverbs 30:7-9

What verse spoke to you in this reading?

Do the New Testament and Old Testament passages have any similarities?

What other verses come to mind as you read these passages?

What questions do you still have? What do you want to know more about? What lesson or theme are you picking up on?

How can you apply these scriptures to your life? -

Today's prayers:

All Access Pass — Day 352

What verse spoke to you in this reading?

Do the New Testament and Old Testament passages have any similarities?

What other verses come to mind as you read these passages?

What questions do you still have? What do you want to know more about? What lesson or theme are you picking up on?

How can you apply these scriptures to your life? -

Today's prayers:

Today's passages:

Habakkuk 1:1-3:19

Revelation 9:1-21

Psalm 137:1-9

Proverbs 30:10

Notes

All Access Pass — Day 353

Today's passages:

Zephaniah 1:1-3:20

Revelation 10:1-11

Psalm 138:1-8

Proverbs 30:11-14

Notes

What verse spoke to you in this reading?

Do the New Testament and Old Testament passages have any similarities?

What other verses come to mind as you read these passages?

What questions do you still have? What do you want to know more about? What lesson or theme are you picking up on?

How can you apply these scriptures to your life? -

Today's prayers:

All Access Pass — Day 354

What verse spoke to you in this reading?
_____
_____
_____

Do the New Testament and Old Testament passages have any similarities?
_____
_____
_____

What other verses come to mind as you read these passages?
_____
_____
_____

What questions do you still have? What do you want to know more about? What lesson or theme are you picking up on?
_____
_____
_____
_____
_____
_____

How can you apply these scriptures to your life? -
_____
_____
_____
_____

Today's prayers:
_____
_____
_____
_____

Today's passages:

Haggai 1:1-2:23

Revelation 11:1-19

Psalm 139:1-24

Proverbs 30:15-16

Notes

All Access Pass — Day 355

Today's passages:

Zechariah 1:1-21

Revelation 12:1-17

Psalm 140:1-13

Proverbs 30:17

Notes

What verse spoke to you in this reading?

Do the New Testament and Old Testament passages have any similarities?

What other verses come to mind as you read these passages?

What questions do you still have? What do you want to know more about? What lesson or theme are you picking up on?

How can you apply these scriptures to your life? -

Today's prayers:

All Access Pass — Day 356

Today's passages:

Zechariah 2:1-3:10

Revelation 13:1-13:18

Psalm 141:1-10

Proverbs 30:18-20

Notes

What verse spoke to you in this reading?

Do the New Testament and Old Testament passages have any similarities?

What other verses come to mind as you read these passages?

What questions do you still have? What do you want to know more about? What lesson or theme are you picking up on?

How can you apply these scriptures to your life? -

Today's prayers:

All Access Pass — Day 357

Today's passages:

Zechariah 4:1-5:11

Revelation 14:1-20

Psalm 142:1-7

Proverbs 30:21-23

Notes

What verse spoke to you in this reading?

Do the New Testament and Old Testament passages have any similarities?

What other verses come to mind as you read these passages?

What questions do you still have? What do you want to know more about? What lesson or theme are you picking up on?

How can you apply these scriptures to your life? -

Today's prayers:

All Access Pass — Day 358

Today's passages:

Zechariah 6:1-7:14

Revelation 15:1-8

Psalm 143:1-12

Proverbs 30:24-28

Notes

What verse spoke to you in this reading?

Do the New Testament and Old Testament passages have any similarities?

What other verses come to mind as you read these passages?

What questions do you still have? What do you want to know more about? What lesson or theme are you picking up on?

How can you apply these scriptures to your life? -

Today's prayers:

All Access Pass — Day 359

Today's passages:

Zechariah 8:1-23

Revelation 16:1-21

Psalm 144:1-15

Proverbs 30:29-31

Notes

What verse spoke to you in this reading?

Do the New Testament and Old Testament passages have any similarities?

What other verses come to mind as you read these passages?

What questions do you still have? What do you want to know more about? What lesson or theme are you picking up on?

How can you apply these scriptures to your life? -

Today's prayers:

All Access Pass — Day 360

Today's passages:

Zechariah 9:1-17

Revelation 17:1-18

Psalm 145:1-21

Proverbs 30:32

Notes

What verse spoke to you in this reading?

Do the New Testament and Old Testament passages have any similarities?

What other verses come to mind as you read these passages?

What questions do you still have? What do you want to know more about? What lesson or theme are you picking up on?

How can you apply these scriptures to your life? -

Today's prayers:

All Access Pass — Day 361

Today's passages:

Zechariah 10:1-11:17

Revelation 18:1-24

Psalm 146:1-10

Proverbs 30:33

Notes

What verse spoke to you in this reading?

Do the New Testament and Old Testament passages have any similarities?

What other verses come to mind as you read these passages?

What questions do you still have? What do you want to know more about? What lesson or theme are you picking up on?

How can you apply these scriptures to your life? -

Today's prayers:

All Access Pass — Day 362

What verse spoke to you in this reading?
_____
_____
_____

Do the New Testament and Old Testament passages have any similarities?
_____
_____
_____

What other verses come to mind as you read these passages?
_____
_____
_____

What questions do you still have? What do you want to know more about? What lesson or theme are you picking up on?
_____
_____
_____
_____
_____
_____

How can you apply these scriptures to your life? -
_____
_____
_____
_____

Today's prayers:
_____
_____
_____
_____

Today's passages:

Zechariah 12:1-13:9

Revelation 19:1-21

Psalm 147:1-20

Proverbs 31:1-7

Notes

All Access Pass — Day 363

Today's passages:

Zechariah 14:1-21

Revelation 20:1-15

Psalm 148:1-14

Proverbs 31:8-9

Notes

What verse spoke to you in this reading?

Do the New Testament and Old Testament passages have any similarities?

What other verses come to mind as you read these passages?

What questions do you still have? What do you want to know more about? What lesson or theme are you picking up on?

How can you apply these scriptures to your life? -

Today's prayers:

All Access Pass — Day 364

Today's passages:

Malachi 1:1-2:17

Revelation 21:1-27

Psalm 149:1-9

Proverbs 31:10-24

What verse spoke to you in this reading?

Do the New Testament and Old Testament passages have any similarities?

What other verses come to mind as you read these passages?

What questions do you still have? What do you want to know more about? What lesson or theme are you picking up on?

How can you apply these scriptures to your life? -

Today's prayers:

All Access Pass — Day 365

Today's passages:

Malachi 3:1-4:6

Revelation 22:1-21

Psalm 150:1-6

Proverbs 31:25-31

Notes

What verse spoke to you in this reading?

Do the New Testament and Old Testament passages have any similarities?

What other verses come to mind as you read these passages?

What questions do you still have? What do you want to know more about? What lesson or theme are you picking up on?

How can you apply these scriptures to your life? -

Today's prayers: